The Real Estate Investors Guide To Getting FAST CASH

A Quick Turn for Big Profits

Craig Picard & Don Goff

Copyright © 2011 by Craig Picard & Don Goff.
All rights reserved.

No part of this publication may be reproduced, store in a retrieval system, or transmitted in any form or by any means, electronic, mechanical, photocopying, recording, scanning, or otherwise, except as permitted under section 107 or 108 of the 1976 United States Copyright Act, without either the prior written permission of the Author.

Limit of Liability/ Disclaimer of Warranty: While the author has used their best efforts in preparing this book, they make no representations or warranties with respect to the accuracy of completeness of the contents of this book and specifically disclaim any implied warranties of merchantability or fitness for a particular purpose. No warranty may be created or extended by sales representatives or written sales materials. The advice and strategies contained herein may not be suitable for your situation. You should consult with a professional where appropriate. The Author shall not be held liable for any loss of profit or any other commercial damages, including but not limited to special, incidental, consequential, or other damages.

For general information on our other products and services, please contact our Customer Care Department at 781-878-7114.

Picard,Craig & Goff,Don
The Real Estate Investors Guide to Getting FAST CASH

ISBN 978-0-615-46537-1

To get the forms discussed in this book and an additional free gift, visit
www.fastcashforms.com

Table of Contents

Chapter 1: Quick Turn Real Estate   7
Target Properties   8
Motivated Sellers   8
Motivational Factors   12

Chapter 2: Marketing   13
Shotgun Marketing   15
Business Cards   16
Flyers   18
Flyer and Business Card Tracking Template   21
Vehicle Signs   22
Bandit Signs   23
Classified Ads   24
Door Hangers   26
Websites   28

Chapter 3: Targeted Marketing   30
Compelling Headlines   36
Construction of the letter   37
Systemizing your targeted marketing   38
Sample Postcards and Letters   42
Targeting Foreclosures   49
Sample Foreclosure Postcards and Letters   50

To get the forms discussed in this book and an additional free gift, visit www.fastcashforms.com

Chapter 4: Relationship Marketing — 64
Which Agents to work with — 67
Questions to ask an Agent — 68

Chapter 5: Pre-Screening Deals — 75
Incoming Call Script — 79
Incoming Call Script Walk Thru — 82
Return Call Script — 88
How to determine if you should meet with the seller — 89

Chapter 6: Equity and Deal Analysis — 94
What is the maximum you can pay — 95
Offer Calculation Worksheet — 96
Definition of Categories — 102
Total Daily Carrying Costs — 105

Chapter 7: Preparing for your visit — 107
Documentation you will need when buying cash — 107
Authorization to Release — 110
Standard Real Estate Purchase and Sale Agreement — 111
Real Estate Disclosure Form — 117
Seller Acknowledgements — 121
Meeting the Seller Checklist — 128
Buying Packet Checklist — 128

To get the forms discussed in this book and an additional free gift, visit www.fastcashforms.com

Chapter 8: Meeting The Homeowner — 129
Credibility Kit Checklist — 131
Property Tour Details — 134
Property Inspection Checklist — 140

Chapter 9: Due Diligence — 143

Chapter 10: Buying "Cash" — 146
Hard Money — 148
Private Money — 149

Chapter 11: Buying "Subject To" — 151

Chapter 12: Buying Lease Option — 152
Lease Option Agreement — 158
Option to Purchase Agreement — 162

Chapter 13: Closing the Deal — 167
12 Steps To Closing — 167

Chapter 14: Selling Quickly — 179
Selling to another investor — 179
Selling to a retail buyer — 180
Which repairs to focus on first? — 186

Accepting Offers — 196
Signing the contract — 198

Chapter 15: Taking The Next Step — 201

To get the forms discussed in this book and an additional free gift, visit www.fastcashforms.com

To get the forms discussed in this book and an additional free gift, visit www.fastcashforms.com

Chapter 1 Quick Turning Real Estate

First we want to thank you for investing in our system. You are wise to make this investment because you are investing in your education, yourself, and your business.

Whether you are a beginner to real estate investing or have been doing this a while, there are always different variations to the way things can be done. It's the tweaks and changes that make a difference.

We have laid out this system from the basics of getting started in quick turn real estate to the advanced, what it takes to get the deal closed by creating a win-win situation. If you are not interested in a win-win situation, then this system and real estate investing is not the place for you.

WHAT IS QUICK TURNING REAL ESTATE

Quick turning real estate is locating motivated sellers, taking control of the property, and selling to another investor or retail buyer. You might be wondering how that is different from flipping properties. The term flipping is a bad word in the real estate industry. The reason it has a negative connotation is that many years ago investors were buying property very cheap that needed a lot of work.

The investor would do some of the work and then sell it to a retail buyer for full retail value. So far no one has done anything wrong. The problem is that the banks that provided the financing to the retail buyer relied on a faulty appraisal. Somehow the appraisal did not reflect the current condition of the property and the lender only found

To get the forms discussed in this book and an additional free gift, visit www.fastcashforms.com

this out when they foreclosed on the property and the property was a mess and would not sell for what was owed on it.

So either the investor influenced the appraiser in some way or the investor was able to hide some of the problems with the property. Either way the banks got hurt by this and made some new lending requirements to avoid this problem. Unfortunately a couple of bad investors spoiled it for everyone else.

Keys to Quick Turning

In order to have a successful quick turn transaction, you must have some key elements:
1. Target the right type of Properties
2. Motivated Seller
3. House that needs repairs or updating (even pretty houses)
4. Significant Equity
5. Seller with a short timeline

TARGET PROPERTIES

One of the first things you need to do as an real estate investor is pick an area that you are going to focus on. There are two main ways you will determine your target area. You will either focus on an area where you have a lot of CASH BUYERS if you are wholesaling or you will select an area that has a lot of Entry level homes since this is the best area to focus on. What are "Entry level homes"? These are homes that a first time home owner will buy. In our area (Rhode Island), this is a 3 bedroom, 1000 square foot ranch or cape.

We like to focus on these types of properties for two main reasons. First of all, a first time home buyer doesn't need to sell a house

To get the forms discussed in this book and an additional free gift, visit www.fastcashforms.com

before he can buy yours. IF you had a buyer that needed to sell his/her house first, there would be a lot more variables, and would overall increase the risk and the time to sell your property. The only thing the first time home buyer needs to wait for is the clear to close from the lender. The second reason is because first time home buyers are the biggest buying pool out there which gives us more people to buy our homes and allows us to sell them quicker. Now that we know what types of homes to focus our energy on let's talk about what type of owners we need to focus on.

MOTIVATED SELLERS

These are the only sellers you will want to work with. If they are not motivated to solve their problems or sell their house quickly, you will waste a lot of time trying to motivate them. There are plenty of motivated sellers out there so you should spend most of your time working with them. If a seller is unmotivated today, it doesn't mean they will stay that way forever. They have not had something that is as strong enough motivation yet. That is why follow up is very important in this business. Sooner or later the person who called you but was not ready to deal with their situation will be. They probably won't call you as you need to follow up with them.

One of the most motivated sellers in this business is someone in foreclosure and this is one niche you want to focus your efforts on. When dealing with people in foreclosures, we have a huge advantage, Time. Time is usually on our side. There is a definite date the homeowner needs to make a decision about what to do. The closer they get to the date, the more motivated they become. Follow up with all the leads until they have either sold the property or solved their problems. Even after they solve their problems you can stay in touch with them by calling or sending a post card from time to time.

To get the forms discussed in this book and an additional free gift, visit www.fastcashforms.com

House that Needs Repairs

Every house needs something; the worse the condition the better the deal in most cases. When a house needs updating or repairs, the seller knows it does and has known for a while that the roof should have been replaced or the gutters cleaned or the carpets replaced. Most times they are limited on cash and had to make the easy choice of feeding the family or repairing the house.

They didn't have the money then and they certainly don't have it now. In most cases they might have some equity in the property but between their financial situation and the condition of the property they are unable to refinance or get a loan to do the repairs. When the property needs repairs, it is much easier to convince them that their house is not worth what it should be because of the updates and repairs it needs. Most sellers don't know how much the repairs will cost but do know it will be more than they can afford.

Pretty houses

Many new investors believe that the only way to make money in this business is by finding distressed properties that need a lot of work. This is one great way to make money as mentioned in the previous section but you can make money quick turning pretty houses as well. On the surface it looks like the reason why there is money to be made is just because it is distressed and it needs work. It's not the fact that the house is in a distressed state that makes the house a potential money maker.

It's the reasons why it is distressed in the first place. The whole reason owners are willing to sell distressed properties at a discount is because they are in a situation and the house being in a distressed state advertises to us there may be a situation. Pretty houses will be a little more challenging because, you won't be able to identify them like you

To get the forms discussed in this book and an additional free gift, visit www.fastcashforms.com

can with distressed properties, you won't be able to use the needed repairs to justify the lower price it will be more dependent on their situation and timeline that will motivate them to sell at a discount.

Significant Equity

In order to quick turn property you need to have significant equity. If there is no equity or little equity and you can't create significant equity through a short sale then you will have trouble buying it and quickly selling for a profit. The more equity, the better because the seller needs some and so don't you. We like to create win-win situations and you need to make sure that the seller is content with what they are getting. Just because there is a lot of equity doesn't mean that you should get it all. When there is significant equity, it opens up more ways to buy the property and you can give them some money today and the rest when the property closes. In essence they are doing either full or partial owner financing. The amount of equity will also determine your buying strategy and exit strategy.

Seller with a Defined Timeline

A seller that has an open ended timeline will not usually have much motivation. Foreclosure is the ultimate situation that has a definition timeline that the seller has no control over. There are many other deadlines that a seller may have and that is why you need to ask why they are selling every time a seller calls. Don't be afraid of asking the question. If the person doesn't provide a deadline you can ask them how quickly they are looking to close. You may need to follow up or press them further to get a deadline from them but those two questions usually help you to determine their deadline.

To get the forms discussed in this book and an additional free gift, visit www.fastcashforms.com

MOTIVATIONAL FACTORS

As mentioned earlier, finding motivated sellers is the key to finding the good deals and making large profits in the business. The more motivated the seller the better the deal you will get. The most motivated sellers are going to be motivated for two reasons either their motivation has compounded because they have more than one problem or as mentioned in the previous section, they have a deadline when they need to sell by. We have shared a list below with many reasons why sellers could be motivated. As you can see there is a lot of opportunity out there.

24 Motivational Factors

- Vacant House
- Condemned Building
- Estate Sale
- Failing Health
- Inherited Property
- Lawsuit
- Retirement
- Bankruptcy
- Expired MLS – Can't Sell
- Title Problems
- Liens
- Foreclosed Properties (i.e. bank reo)
- Pre-foreclosure
- Relocation
- Divorce
- Failed Rehab
- Failed Business
- Loss of Job
- Mismanaged Rental
- Job Transfer
- Death in Family
- Code Violations
- Interest Rate Adjustment
- Negative Cash flow

To get the forms discussed in this book and an additional free gift, visit www.fastcashforms.com

Chapter 2: Marketing

Any business person will tell you that marketing is the key for a successful business. The real estate investing business is no exception. In order to market effectively, you need to be focused and always adding more marketing to you business in order to increase income. Once you have one or two marketing campaigns that you are managing, then you will need to track your marketing.

With this product, we will cover the best strategies for today's real estate marketplace for getting started.   These strategies will allow you to easily identify motivated sellers. Motivated sellers are required to quickly make money in real estate. Motivated sellers will sell their property for less than market value because they need a quick solution. You have heard the saying, "Time is Money" using the right marketing techniques at the right time will make you enable you to increase the profits in real estate.

Here's the Million Dollar question: **What is the best Marketing Technique?**

This is a question that we get over and over again and the answer we always give is that we can show you ten ways to find one deal but not one way to find ten. Marketing is a moving target. It constantly changes and you need to always be trying new things. One month it could be Bandit signs and the next month it could be direct mail.

You should always be educating yourself on marketing and trying new things. Your goal when you're getting started should be implementing at least one new marketing technique or campaign every month so that you are using multiple strategies at all times.

Another common question we get is…. "What types of marketing should you start with? Start with the simple and cheap marketing techniques first. Simple because when you are getting

To get the forms discussed in this book and an additional free gift, visit www.fastcashforms.com

started, we want you to be able to implement the most amounts of campaigns in the least amount or time and build momentum.

Cheap because we found that the low cost marketing methods work just as well if not better than some of the higher cost ones and by coaching many investors we found that many of them use the cost of marketing as an excuse for not getting started so we like to eliminate that as one of your excuses so you can JUST GET STARTED.. This system will show you that you can be successful in this business with very little money, and keep your overhead low until you cash your first few checks and are building momentum.

There are three types of Marketing; shotgun, target marketing, and relationship marketing.

The one you should focus on from day one is shotgun marketing. This type of marketing is what is going to allow you to get a quick start at a low cost and you will be able to implement this one the fastest. In parallel you should be working on your relationship marketing since it is free and all it will cost you is a little of your time. Shortly after you get your shotgun marketing started, you should also start your Target Marketing campaign (Direct mail). It is a little more of an investment but you can also get a great response from it.

Your Ultimate Marketing Goal is GETTING MOTIVATED SELLERS TO CALL YOU. The only way you get them to call you is by getting your marketing out there. Not sure if you've heard this before or realize this but make no mistake about it you are not in the Real Estate Business you are in the MARKETING BUSINESS. Whether you are marketing for CASH BUYERS or for potential deals, this is the single most important part of the business and the one you should be devoting at least 40 percent of you time on it.

Without marketing you can't operate the rest of your business, marketing is the foundation from which the rest of you real estate investing business is built. Focusing on marketing is what will ensure your long term success in the business. In the upcoming sections we are

To get the forms discussed in this book and an additional free gift, visit www.fastcashforms.com

going to share with you all the top marketing methods you should be using to get your phone ringing off the hook.

SHOTGUN MARKETING

What is Shotgun marketing? These are marketing techniques that expose your services to a large audience. The idea is to broadcast a message (our message is WE BUY HOUSES), that will reach the largest number of people possible. By reaching the largest audience possible exposure to the product is maximized. We are going to cover the cheapest most affective techniques which are Business Cards, Flyers, Car signs, Bandit Signs, Door Hangers, and Classified Ads.

To get the forms discussed in this book and an additional free gift, visit www.fastcashforms.com

BUSINESS CARDS

We Buy Houses
$ CASH $ or Take over Payments

We Close Faster....

Choice Home Buyers
Craig Picard ~ Real Estate Investor   Mobile: 401-555-xxxx
2130 Mendon Road   Toll Free: 877-789-xxxx
Suite 3, # 372   Fax: 877-574-xxxx
Cumberland RI 02864   Email:Craig@abcxxx.com

See Back

- Unwanted House?   • Foreclosure?
- Need To Sell Quickly?   • Divorcing?
- Behind on Payments?   • Relocating?
- Bad Tenants?   • Fire Damage?

These are common problems that can happen to anyone!

We buy houses from people in situations just like yours in any area or price range and we can close quickly. We are not acting as Real Estate Brokers. We are Real Estate Investors and do not charge commissions or fees. You'll get a quick sale, we'll handle all the paperwork (with no hassles) and we'll help you put your worries behind you.

➢ We can pay **Cash Fast!**   ➢ We can **Take Over** Payments!
➢ We can **Stop Forclosure!**   ➢ We can make **Back** Payments!

P.S. Rarely do problems just go away. Call NOW! Let us help you find a solution! (877)789-XXXX or (401)555-XXXX

  Business cards are one of the cheapest forms of marketing and they get results. As you can see with the example above you can jam a lot of information on the front and back of a card. I really consider

To get the forms discussed in this book and an additional free gift, visit www.fastcashforms.com

them a miniature version of a billboard. You can get the same message across but they cost a lot less money.

When you design your card, it doesn't have to be the same as the one above but make sure you have a similar design. Make sure you use a color that will stand out like Yellow, Green, or Pink. In addition to color there are certain things you need to have on your card to get people to call you. See the list below.

Front

- WE BUY HOUSES – Catches their Attention
- CASH – Tells them you Can Close Quick
- Your Information – So they can contact you

Back

- A list of the types of properties you buy
- What Services you offer
- How you can solve their problem
- Call NOW – Everyone needs a call to action

Another advantage of business cards is that they are small and easily portable so you can have them with you at all times. Why is this important? Well, if they are in your wallet or purse you can be marketing every day. You should be giving a business card to everyone you meet and everywhere you go you should be putting out your business Card.

Your goal should be to put out 10-15 business cards a day. Many places that you go to on a regular basis have peg/cork boards. You might not have noticed this before but you will now.
We have listed 11 of the best place that have peg boards. If they don't have peg boards don't be afraid to leave some in shopping carts, on the window sill, or on a shelf somewhere.

People will call you. We've also listed some creative places that work as well.

To get the forms discussed in this book and an additional free gift, visit www.fastcashforms.com

Places with Peg Boards

- With the Bill at Restaurants
- Restaurants
- Pizza Parlors
- Barber Shops
- Post office
- Home Depot
- Lowes
- Paint Stores
- Supply Houses
- Sub Shops
- Supermarkets Banks

Creative Places

- With the Bill at Restaurants
- Mail them with Utility Bills
- Phone Booths
- Mail Them with Direct Mail
- Leave on Pump at Gas Stations
- Put in "How to Sell Your Home" Books at the Book Store

FLYERS

Flyers are another way to get a lot of exposure with a small investment. Just like business cards, Flyers can be placed on all the pegboards where you place your cards. If you don't ask, you don't get. In addition to the peg boards there are some other great marketing methods with flyers.

To get the forms discussed in this book and an additional free gift, visit www.fastcashforms.com

You can go door to door in Neighborhoods you are farming, put them in the middle of newspapers where everyone can see them, put them on cars in parking lots or pass them out at events. Below we have shared some ***Tricks of the Trade***.

Peg Boards

- **Tabs:** Make sure to put tabs on the bottom of the flyer with your number. **Nugget**- Make sure you rip one off because no one likes to be the 1st one to pull a tab off.
- **On Door:** At gas stations and sub shops ask if you can put them on the entrance door.

Newspaper

- **Advertising**: Have multiple local businesses put ads on the back of the flyer to pay for the cost.
- **Paper**: Use colored paper so it stands out

Parking Lots

- **Door**: Put them in door handle instead of door. This will lessen the chance of them ending up on the ground.
- **Pick up**: Go back a few hours after you flyer and pick up flyers on the ground.

To get the forms discussed in this book and an additional free gift, visit www.fastcashforms.com

WE BUY HOUSES

Need to Sell Your Property Quickly?
"Or Know Some One Who Does"? ($1000 Referral Fee)

Unwanted House or Relocating?
Facing Foreclosure?
Tired of Tenants?
Behind on Payments?
Selling an Estate?

Advantages!

Your Property Can be sold in **48 HOURS**!
NO WAITING while it sits on the Market!
No Worries about repairs or maintenance **LESS STRESS!**
You will know the bottom line price with **NO SURPRISES!**

How Can We Help?

We can pay **CASH FAST**!
We can Stop **FORECLOSURE**!
We can close **QUICKLY** w/ **NO HASSLES**!
We can **handle** all the paperwork!

Call NOW!
401-555-5785 or 877-555-5785
www.yourwebsite.com

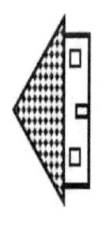

| 877-555-5785 |
| Your Company |

877-555-5785
Your Company

877-555-5785
Your Company

877-555-5785
Your Company

877-555-5785
Your Company

877-555-5785
Your Company

401-555-5785
Your Company

401-555-5785
Your Company

401-555-5785
Your Company

401-555-5785
Your Company

401-555-5785
Your Company s

401-555-5785
Your Company

To get the forms discussed in this book and an additional free gift, visit
www.fastcashforms.com

FLYER AND BUSINESS CARD TRACKING TEMPLATE

DATE	Location	Flyer/ Cards	Comments	Followup Date	Comments
			Flyer Tracking		
11/28/10	EXAMPLE Lil General 263 Diamond hill rd cumb	F	Let me post in window. Said owner wouldn't allow any advertising	12/28/10	

To get the forms discussed in this book and an additional free gift, visit www.fastcashforms.com

VEHICLE SIGNS

WE BUY HOUSES
$ CASH $
401-555-HOME

WE BUY HOUSES
$ CASH $
401-555-HOME

We Buy Houses
$ CASH $
401-555-HOME
877-555-HOME

    Magnetic signs are cheap and easy to install. You should place signs on both the driver's side and passenger's side of your vehicle. A good size that fit most cars is 22" x 10". Also, smaller signs that are about the size of a bumper sticker (11" x 5.5") can fit on the back of your car. If you have a SUV or a Caravan then you can have a vinyl sign on your back window like the one below. The message should be clear and visible to other cars driving by you. For instance, "WE BUY HOUSES" with a phone number.

    Also, why limit the signs to just your vehicle? What about your family and friends? Would they be interested in $1000 if a house is purchased from the signs that someone saw on their car or truck? How about your contractors? I have a painter that had no signs for his business on his vehicles. So I asked him if he would put my signs on his vehicles. He now travels with my signs on two of his trucks.

    Sure your friends may make fun of you and your traveling billboard, but in the end, it is the leads that are generated and those leads

To get the forms discussed in this book and an additional free gift, visit www.fastcashforms.com

that turn into deals. The only one laughing in the end will be yourself and the owner of the vehicle when you a cashing big checks.

BANDIT SIGNS

Bandit signs are another way to market your business inexpensively. Bandit signs should be one of the first forms of marketing that you should implement. When I say bandit sign, I mean the signs you see affixed to telephone poles or on exit ramps. I don't know why they call them bandit signs. Perhaps it is because you feel like a bandit as you are hanging the signs in the pre-dawn hours under the cover of darkness. Yes, we hang these signs in the pre-dawn hours, but it is because this is the time with the least amount of traffic and we find it easier to put the signs where you want at this time.

The types of signs we use are corrugated plastic signs. We use 12" x 18" signs and 18" x 24" signs. Our signs are yellow and black, but you can customize these to any colors you want as you can see in the examples on this page. Make sure to brand yourself by matching all your forms of signs. Some of the best signs are the simplest signs. A sign that we have gotten a good with is "WE BUY HOUSES", "CASH", with our phone number.

You should use something similar to this. The first weekend we put up thirty signs, many of them came down right away. Even though a large percentage of the signs came down quickly, from those thirty signs we did get about twenty phone calls. With this high response, we

To get the forms discussed in this book and an additional free gift, visit www.fastcashforms.com

quickly realized that we needed to schedule time to get more signs up and cover more territory. You should have a system where you put up signs a few times a month. Once you get a system in place delegate this task to someone else and spend your time on building your business. Below we have shared some *Tricks of the Trade*.

- **Corrugation:** Order the signs with horizontal corrugation so the signs won't bend in half with the wind. This will save you time and money since won't have to go out and replace signs that bend in half.
- **Height:** Put them up as high as possible as they will stay up the longest.
- **Placement:** Best place to put your signs are at highway off ramps, at intersections in high traffic areas, and in the yard of properties you own and of yards of friends and family. From time to time you will get a call from a city official to take down your signs. Make sure to pull down your signs when they call. One way to lessen the chance of getting a call is by not flooding any specific town with your signs which means don't put a sign up every intersection you see.

CLASSIFIED ADS

We Buy HOUSES	**Need to SELL**
Any Condition/Situation With no Hassles	We Have **Options!**
We Close Faster!	We buy houses/land Any Condition/Situation
Call Craig 877-789-4663 www.abchomes.com	We Close Faster!! Call 24 hours 401-555-4663 www.ABChomes.com

To get the forms discussed in this book and an additional free gift, visit www.fastcashforms.com

Placing newspaper classified ads is a little higher investment then business cards, flyers, and signs but they work so you want to add this marketing technique at some point. You might have noticed that we have said investment and not cost. This is because this is the mindset you need to have to be successful at marketing.

Every marketing dollar you spend is not an expense it's an investment in your business and what you want to do is get a return on your investment. If it costs you $2000/year to place your ad and you get two wholesale deals off of it and make $10k that's a 400% return. Who wouldn't take that? I would trade $2k for $10k any day.

How would you like a place where you can put your Classified AD for FREE? Have you ever heard of an internet website called Craigslist, www.craigslist.com ? This is a great place to put your ad. Put your ad under "Real Estate for Sale" and under "Real Estate Wanted" . Included on this page are some examples of Classified Ads. Here's another tip, you can post your ad to another online site in addition to craigslist www.backpage.com .

You should place you ad's right NOW, don't wait. It only takes a few minutes to do, it's FREE, and remember people don't know you are out there unless you are advertising so this is a great way to get started right away.

To get the forms discussed in this book and an additional free gift, visit www.fastcashforms.com

```
┌─────────────────────────────┐
│      We Buy Houses          │
│        $ CASH $             │
│   Any Area, Any Condition   │
│      We Close Faster!       │
│   Call NOW! 401-555-4663    │
│      www.abchomes.com       │
│                             │
└─────────────────────────────┘
```

DOOR HANGERS

As we mentioned in the beginning of this manual, one of the first things you need to do as an real estate investor is pick an area that you are going to focus on. The best areas to focus on are areas with entry level homes. Once select the area you are going to farm, you want to know that area inside and out. Once of the best ways to do this is to drive the area. When you are driving the area there are a few things you want to do.

You want to notice the following: which realtors for sale signs you keep seeing over and over again (these are realtors you want to build relationships with), which houses have for sale by owner signs (these are phone numbers you want to call), and distressed properties (these are properties you want to put door hangers on). Here are some reasons why door hangers work well: They catch the owners attention when they visit the property and are not easily missed, the homeowner doesn't have to open anything and they immediately see your message, and they are personal since a lot of home owners will think you personally stopped by which gives them a better chance of calling.

To get the forms discussed in this book and an additional free gift, visit www.fastcashforms.com

Your door hanger should be a bright color like your business cards and should have verbiage like the sample below so they know how you can help solve their problem.

To get the forms discussed in this book and an additional free gift, visit www.fastcashforms.com

WEBSITES

In the business world today websites are a must. If you don't have a website, it is less likely that people will not trust you. Besides building credibility and describing your company's services, your website is a great place to pre-screen leads. Your website should be on every piece of marketing material that you send out.

The great thing about the World Wide Web is that it is available 24 hours per day seven days a week. When you are sleeping it is working for you. We have had many sellers contact us through our website rather than calling us. Some people are afraid of the phone or are not sure what will happen when they call. Others are unable to deal with their problems during the day and spend many sleepless nights searching the internet for a solution.

Make sure that your website has a qualifying page that has the same sort of qualifying questions that the incoming call script has. The qualifying page is where you will direct them to go so they won't end up at your main page and be lost and confused. If your site provides an easy way for them to leave their contact information you will have success. Keep your qualifying page as short as possible.

I know you want to know everything about them but they may not want to take the time to fill it out. Get the essential details that you need on the website and when you speak to them live, you can get the rest of your questions answered.

To get the forms discussed in this book and an additional free gift, visit www.fastcashforms.com

To get the forms discussed in this book and an additional free gift, visit www.fastcashforms.com

Chapter 3: Targeted Marketing

Direct mail is one of our favorite methods of marketing. Along with some of the inexpensive shotgun methods direct mail should be one of your first marketing techniques you focus on. With direct mail you can select groups of prospects that you want to target and market to them directly. The great part about it is that once you send out the letters, you can be out doing other marketing while you wait for them to call.

The basic components of a direct mail campaign include targeting a list of prospects to mail to, creating a message to fit that target, and giving them a compelling reason to call you. One thing you want to note is direct mail only works if the recipient opens the envelope and reads what is inside. This section will focus on what you need to do to make direct mail work for your business.

How to get Started

When starting a direct mail campaign, the first thing you want to do is to select the prospects that you want to target. Our targets are going to be people who either have specific motivational factors or live an area or neighborhood where we farming so we can cover any situation they are in. Below is a list of groups of people to target and why they have a greater chance of being motivated.

- **Pre-Foreclosure**: Have financial situation and have deadline to correct it
- **Vacant or Distressed:** Either don't have money to do repairs or detached themselves from the property.
- **Building Code Violations:** Don't have money to make repairs and are tired of getting phone calls and fines from building officials.

To get the forms discussed in this book and an additional free gift, visit www.fastcashforms.com

- **Out of Town Owners**: Inherited unwanted house, Absentee landlord
- **Expired Listings:** Lost belief of someone being able to sell their property.
- **Free and Clear:** Houses are dated and know hard to sell. Typically have equity
- **Divorce:** Just want to split ties ASAP . Don't want it to take 3-6months to sell.
- **Tired Land Lords:** Sick of Dealing with Tenants

How to get a Direct Mail List

There are two main ways to get a list either create one, or buy one from a list broker. Below are the ways to find lists of the targeted prospects so you can get your mailing campaigns started. In addition, here are some list broker resources you can use:
www.melissadata.com, http://www.listsource.com , www.infousa.com .

- **Pre-Foreclosure**: Local Newspaper, court house, list broker
- **Vacant or Distressed:** Farm your area and make a list of all distressed properties
- **Building Code Violations:** Local Building Official/Inspector Office
- **Out of Town Owners**: Tax Assessor or List broker
- **Expired Listings:** MLS, or Realtor who you have a relationship with
- **Free and Clear:** List Broker
- **Divorce:** Probate Court
- **Tired Land Lords:** Call For Rent Signs, Eviction Court

To get the forms discussed in this book and an additional free gift, visit www.fastcashforms.com

Post Card or Envelope

Now that we have a list the next step is to get our marketing started by sending our prospects their first piece of mail. A direct mail campaign can be done using either letters or post cards. Post cards work well because you don't have to worry about the homeowner opening the envelope. Most people will sort their mail over the trash can or paper shredder and throw away or shred anything that looks like junk mail. Post cards do a great job of capturing the attention of the homeowner if they include a compelling headline and create interest that will compel them to read the rest of the text.

The drawback of the post card is that you have limited space to tell your story and get the homeowner to call.

When specifically targeting foreclosures using post cards creates another issue: Post cards don't need to be opened and therefore lack confidentiality. Anyone who sees the post card in the homeowner's mail will now know that they are in foreclosure or will start to ask questions. Some people are embarrassed by the situation and they don't want anyone to know. What if someone other than the homeowner gets the mail such as the spouse who did not know that their house was in foreclosure?

Post cards are a good tool to use towards the end of the process when there is only a few weeks left and you have not been able to contact them any other way. If you use post cards early in the process, you can try something that catches their attention but doesn't specifically mention foreclosure.

Most of the homeowners want to try to save their house and stay in it during the early stages of the process and refinance is a solution most are familiar with but may not think that they qualify or that it is an

To get the forms discussed in this book and an additional free gift, visit www.fastcashforms.com

option for them. When you are targeting foreclosures be more of a solutions provider rather than just trying to buy their house.

Envelope

The first step in getting a letter opened is slipping below the radar of the homeowner who is detecting junk mail and destroying it. It all starts with the type of envelope and how it looks on the outside. You should use a Number 10 envelope and hand address every envelope in blue ink putting your return address label in the upper left hand corner and using a live stamp.

Special Envelope

If you really want to go further and get past their junk mail defenses, you could use a square envelope. The homeowner might think it is an invitation which they actually are an invitation to purchase your service, and they will be more inclined to open the envelope.

How not to Address an Envelope

When you think of what causes you to not open a piece of mail but rather shred it, or throw it away, the following come to mind:

Labels
Metered postage
Business name in the upper left corner
Computer generated names and addresses on the envelope
Bulk rate, (most will not be delivered in a timely fashion)
Envelopes with windows

These are the things you want to avoid when doing your direct mail.

To get the forms discussed in this book and an additional free gift, visit www.fastcashforms.com

Delegate

You should be delegating or outsourcing these menial tasks to someone else. You should be able to find someone to stamp, stuff, and address an envelope for 13-15 cents per envelope and that is a small price to pay to free up your time. With that free time you will be able to go find other deals. Anytime you can delegate something that you can easily train someone else to do, something that is not a good use of your time, or something that typically becomes a second priority to something else then do it.

For example, if you have a homeowner call you and say they want to sell and the property has significant equity or you have some envelopes to address and stuff that evening, which are you going to do? Of course, go see the property. That's the problem most investors have is that once they get a lead on a deal and start working it, they stop marketing and then after they do the deal they have to get the names going again.

Once you learn to learn to outsource and delegate, your business will grow by leaps and bounds because the pump is always primed and the deals are flowing from it. If you insist on doing this yourself as you get into this business, make sure that you are doing this task while watching television at night or other non business time and set a goal for when you will delegate this function.

What day should you send mailings?

Set up your schedule to have the mail delivered on Tuesday, Wednesday, or Thursday. In most cases people are not going to deal with their problems on the weekend so you need to get their attention prior to their weekend plans to relax. On Monday they are trying to

To get the forms discussed in this book and an additional free gift, visit www.fastcashforms.com

recuperate from the weekend and are too busy with getting their work week going. Having the mail delivered on a Tuesday, Wednesday, or Thursday will increase your response rate.

This doesn't mean these are the only three days of the week to operate your business; it only applies to direct mail. Take a look at your own situation and see if your mail tends to pile up over the weekend.

Mission Accomplished the Envelope has been Opened

Now that you have gotten the homeowner to open the envelope, they will take the next two seconds to decide whether or not to read the rest of it or throw it away. In that two seconds you need to grab their attention and give them a reason to read your message. You must have a bold compelling headline that answers the question, "What is in it for me?"

How to Create a Compelling Headline

Your headline is the most important part of your direct mail piece. If the headline does not entice them to read further, it doesn't matter what the rest of the letter says because they will never see it.

Elements of a Great Headline

    Attract attention
    Stimulate curiosity and intrigue
    Reveal the strongest benefit of your offer
    Must make news, be seen as new or different
    Must be specific and meaningful to our prospect

To get the forms discussed in this book and an additional free gift, visit www.fastcashforms.com

COMPELLING HEADLINES

"We Buy Houses Any Area, Any Condition FAST Closings!"

Who Else Wants to Sell Their House in 7 Days or Less!

Selling Soon? Highest Prices Paid For Your Real Estate!

Who Else wants to sell their house Fast with no Hassles?

*"Stop Your Upcoming Foreclosure In Nine Days Or Less…
Don't Let the Bank Take Your Property!"*

"Are You Drowning In A Sea Of Debt"

*"Who Else wants to Hear
Options that the Bank didn't tell them about?"*

"STOP YOUR FORECLOSURE NOW!"

Can you see how these headlines are designed to grab the reader's attention and entice them to read on? If you were someone who was in foreclosure and frustrated with your situation, wouldn't you call so that you can make the pain stop?

This is why the headline is the most important part of any direct mail piece. When using a post card you can use the same technique to capture attention by putting the headline in the front and instruct them to turn the card over to learn more.

Now that you understand the basics of the headline, you should write out 5-10 headlines. Go through the list and choose the ones that

*To get the forms discussed in this book and an additional free gift, visit
www.fastcashforms.com*

are the most compelling and attention grabbing. The ones that scream, "I've got to have that!" are the headlines to use. The key to creating headlines is to look through the newspapers and magazines and book or magazine covers to get more ideas.

You may even find a current event and tie your message to that. Remember, headlines are designed to do one thing, get the reader to read the first sentence of the body of the letter.

CONSTRUCTION OF THE LETTER

First Line

The purpose of the first sentence is to get them to read the next sentence and so on. The first sentence should describe the problem they are facing. This will remind them of the pain but will keep them reading because they read that you have the solution.

Body

The remainder of the body of the letter will focus on what they will get when doing business with you. Let them know that you can do something remarkable. Make the benefits impossible to ignore.

Credibility

Once you have stated that you can do something, you need to remove the doubt from their minds. They are thinking that is not possible but you need to prove that you are credible. There are two primary ways that you can show credibility. The first is to be a member of the Better Business Bureau and the second is to provide a testimonial from someone that you have helped in their situation. You

---

To get the forms discussed in this book and an additional free gift, visit www.fastcashforms.com

will need to get permission to use their name because you always want to put it at the end of the testimonial.

Sense of Urgency

You need to create a sense of urgency with the homeowner. A well crafted headline and first sentence, and body of the letter will be useless without telling them what to do next. To stop foreclosure, pick up the phone and **Call Me Now!** These people are looking for someone to guide them, to tell them what to do.

The Last Part of the Letter – P.S.

The P.S. is probably the second most important part of the letter. The first is the headline and the second is the P.S. When the homeowner opens the letter, the first thing they see is the headline then they immediately look down to the bottom to see who sent them the letter. When they look to the bottom they will see your name and the P.S. will catch their attention. The P.S. should restate the problem, restate the most desirable benefit and end with another call to action. You can also add a special bonus like, "Call now for your free report on how to stop foreclosure in 7 days or less".

SYSTEMIZING YOUR TARGETED MARKETING

Testing You Mail Piece

You should test all marketing that you use for this business. Direct mail happens to be the easiest to test because it is low cost per piece and it is more easily measured because you know how many went out, how many were returned undelivered, and finally the number who

To get the forms discussed in this book and an additional free gift, visit www.fastcashforms.com

responded. Measuring results by mailing to one target audience such as homeowners in foreclosure is essential. If you are sending out to different type of groups like bankruptcy, Foreclosure, pre-notice of default, divorce, your results will be skewed.

After you have sent out at least 500 letters, track and record the results. This will be your control group of the test. Now you can change the marketing piece to see what the results are. If the results are better, then change your marketing to the new piece. Make sure that you do not change multiple items in the letter or you will have no way of knowing which item improved or decreased the response rate.

TRACKING YOUR MARKETING

It always amazes us how much money investors spend on marketing and never track the results. Okay, we were guilty of this as well when we first started. The reason we started to track was our marketing budget became increasingly high because we continued to add marketing campaigns but did not know which ones were producing.

We were doing plenty of business from the marketing that we were doing, but was some of the marketing a waste of money? Luckily for me I started to track my marketing and this allowed me to tweak my marketing to get better results. What started as an exercise to limit the marketing budget turned into spending more on the right type of marketing. We were okay with spending more because we either eliminated the weak performers or adjusted the message and increased our response rate.

Not only were we spending slightly more money, we increased the amount of business dramatically. Your competition is not doing this so you need to track and evaluate the marketing that you are putting out. You do not need an elaborate system to track your results.

To get the forms discussed in this book and an additional free gift, visit www.fastcashforms.com

Either color code each letter or put a tracking number somewhere in the letter. When the prospect calls, just ask them to read the color or number to you and document it. You can use a spreadsheet to track the results and after sending at least 350-500 pieces of the same letter, you will have a good idea if it is working.

Pro's and Con's of Direct Mail

PRO'S

- It's targeted marketing
- You can reach people that you may not have a phone number for and they don't live in the property
- Easy to Systemize
- Easy to Delegate or Outsource
- Requires little time for the amount of leads it generates
- Can do right from your office
- Low Cost compared to some other forms of marketing
- High ROI

CON'S

- Response rate is typically around 1%
- Less personable
- Many pieces of mail just never get opened
- Need to send several pieces and remain consistent for it to work

How many letters do I send?

Many new investors will attempt direct mail but will get discouraged quick because they send out two mailings don't land a deal so they give up. What they don't realize is that it has been proven that in most cases the average sale is made after the fourth follow-up. It's

To get the forms discussed in this book and an additional free gift, visit www.fastcashforms.com

not to say that you won't get any deals in your first three mailings you send out. What it means is keep mailing if you don't.

You will need a sample size of at least 150 mail pieces in order to determine if a mail campaign is working or not. The most important thing is to track your results.

When you start mailing to a new list of names you want to hit them hard at the beginning so they get use to seeing your mailings and then start spreading out your mailings. Remember with time every seller's circumstances will change and you want to be the one they think of when they are ready to sell.

Here's what we have found to work well. If we are buying a list we typically like to start with a post card to test the list to verify addresses are good.

Next we follow-up with letters and postcards. It's good to switch it up and track what your getting your best response from. Below is the timeline of a typical campaign and how you should spread out your mailings.

Step 1: PC
Step 2: PC or Letter   1 week later
Step 3: PC or Letter 2 weeks later
Step 4: PC or Letter 1 month later
Step 5 : PC or Letter 1 months later
Step 6 : PC or Letter Every 3 months

To get the forms discussed in this book and an additional free gift, visit www.fastcashforms.com

SAMPLE POSTCARDS and LETTERS
(Works for all Types)

ABC Real Estate Solutions, LLC
45 Benefit Street
Providence, RI 02909

Address Service Requested

Who Else Wants To Sell Their House in 7 Days or Less?
CALL NOW!
(401) 555-4663 or (877) 555-4661

WE BUY HOUSES!
Any Situation, Condition - NO HASSLES

Dear Property Owner:

We are a <u>Local</u> Real Estate Company that buys houses and multi-families. We can pay all cash, close in days with no hassles, and handle all the paperwork.

We noticed your property at:

If interested in selling this property or any other property, please call our office at (401) 555-4663 or visit us at www.abchomes.com.

Ask for Craig/Don or leave a message and we will return your call as soon as possible. We would appreciate a call one way or another so we know you received this card. Take Action & Call TODAY!

P.S. For your Free Report entitled "How to sell your House in 7 Days or Less" Visit us at www.abchomes.com

BBB MEMBER RHODE ISLAND

ABC Real Estate Solutions, LLC
401-555-4663
877-555-4661

To get the forms discussed in this book and an additional free gift, visit www.fastcashforms.com

ABC Real Estate Solutions, LLC
45 Benefit Street
Providence, RI 02909

Address Service Requested

To get the forms discussed in this book and an additional free gift, visit www.fastcashforms.com

(DIVORCE LETTER)

Selling Soon?
Highest Prices Paid For Your Real Estate!

Jane and Joe Smith
123 Main St.
Any Town, USA

Dear Jane and Joe,

I'm a real estate investor looking to buy properties in your neighborhood. I'm contacting local homeowners
in the hopes that you may be interested in selling your property to me.

I'm part of a group that buys between five and 10 houses per months and would like to buy your house
next. I can either close quickly or take as much time as you like.

This is what will happen when you call me: I'll come over and take a look at your house. Next I'll compare
it to other similar houses that have recently sold in the area. I will then offer you a fair price to purchase
your property.

It's that simple. No aggressive realtors to deal with, no "For Sale" sign in front of your house; and no
parade of people coming through your house at all hours of the day, night and weekends, checking out all of
your stuff and asking you questions that are none of their business anyway.

To get the forms discussed in this book and an additional free gift, visit www.fastcashforms.com

To find out what I can offer you for your house, call me now at 555-5555. I look forward to our speaking.

Sincerely,

Craig Picard

P.S. – For a quick, quiet, confidential sale of your property, call me now **at 555-5555.**

(Out of Town Owner Letter)

(City) Investor Looking To Buy Your (City) Property

Dear Friend,

I'm an investor who buys property in the (City) area and notice on the tax records that you own one or more properties in this area.

I'd like to buy your property at a fair price.

If you have any interest in selling or just exploring what you might be able to get for your property, give me a call so that we can discuss it.

There are many reasons why someone may be interested in selling a property, family matters, inherited an unwanted property, cash flow issues, tired of ownership…the list goes on.

If you find yourself interested in selling, I'm interested in buying. I'm not acting as a realtor, I'm a buyer, call me now at 555-5555 to discuss the possibilities.

To get the forms discussed in this book and an additional free gift, visit www.fastcashforms.com

Sincerely,

Craig Picard

P.S. To find out what I would buy your property for, call me now at 555-5555!

We Buy Houses
Any Area, Any Condition
Fast Closings!

Property Owner
73 Dawn Blvd
Woonsocket, RI 02895

Are you or is anyone you know looking to sell a property quickly?

I'm a local investor looking to purchase real estate in your area. I am interested in any property, whether it is in need of a lot of repair or in "move-in" condition.

I'm willing to pay a fair market price and can close quickly or take as long as you want.

How does this work? Simply call me at 401-555-4663, I'll come out and take a look at the property, I'll compare it to similar properties that have sold in the area and make you an offer.

As I stated before, I have the ability to pay cash and close quickly. For a **free** evaluation of your property, or if you want to tell me about

To get the forms discussed in this book and an additional free gift, visit www.fastcashforms.com

somebody else's property (I'll give you a cash bonus if I buy it!), call me now at 401-555-4663.

I look forward to our speaking.

Kindest regards,

Craig Picard

P.S. For a fast closing and a fair price for your property (or someone's who you know), call me now at 401-555-4663.

(Expired Listings, Distressed) Who Else Wants to Sell Their House in 7 Days or Less!

Property Owner
124 Dawn Blvd
Woonsocket, RI 02895

    I'm a local Real Estate investor looking to purchase real estate in your area. I am interested in your property. Please let me know if you are interested in selling.

    I have the ability to pay cash and close quickly. For a **free** evaluation of your property, or if you want to tell me about somebody else looking to sell their property (I'll give you a cash bonus if I buy it!), call me at 401-555-4663.

Here are some of the benefits of selling directly to me.

To get the forms discussed in this book and an additional free gift, visit www.fastcashforms.com

- I can purchase your property in its "AS IS" condition. No professional inspections, updating or repairs necessary.
- I can buy your house as fast or as slow as you need us to.
- You can avoid paying a 5-6% real estate commission.

I look forward to our speaking.

                                    Kindest regards,

                                    Don Goff

P.S. For a Hassle free closing and a fair price for your property, call me now at
401-555-4663.

(distressed , vacant or code violations)
Has Your Property Become A Headache?
I've Got The Cure…

Joan Redding
45 Eddy Street
Providence, RI 02909

Dear Joan,

      How would you like to get rid of the biggest headache that you have in your life right now? That's right, I'm talking about your property.

      If you're ready to sell, I'm ready to buy. I'm an investor in your area who specializes in properties like yours…properties with problems.

      Have you had enough of paying high taxes, insurance, and the city officials calling to complain ? Are you tired of making repairs to things that you didn't damage?

To get the forms discussed in this book and an additional free gift, visit www.fastcashforms.com

Sometimes people buy properties and don't realize what they've gotten themselves into. Sometimes people buy properties knowing what they're getting into but just get tired of dealing with it.

I'm ready to give you a fair price for your property if you're ready to sell. Call me now at 401-555-466 3and I'll rid you of your headache.

>Sincerely,

>Craig Picard

P.S. – For a quick, painless sale of your property, call me now at 401-555-4663!

P.P.S.S. – I'm an investor looking to **buy your property** -- I'm not a sales agent looking to list it!

TARGETING FORECLOSURES

Foreclosure Mailings

How many letters to send will depend largely on the amount of time between when you get the list of names and when the foreclosure auction is scheduled to take place. You want them to receive at least one piece a week and as many as two pieces in seven days. The reason you have to send so many is because you don't know when they will open it. If they open it, your message may not have been right for them at the time. You need to be consistent because you don't know what will cause them to react.

Here is an example if you have 60 days:

>Step 1 letter
>Step 2 letter   3 days later
>Step 3 letter   4 days later
>Step 4 letter   3 days later

To get the forms discussed in this book and an additional free gift, visit www.fastcashforms.com

Step 5 letter 4 days later
Step 6 letter 3 days later
Step 7 letter 4 days later
Step 8 letter 3 days later

SAMPLE POST CARDS AND LETTERS
(Foreclosure)

ABC Real Estate Solutions, LLC
45 Benefit Street
Providence, RI 02909

Address Service Requested

To get the forms discussed in this book and an additional free gift, visit www.fastcashforms.com

ABC Real Estate Solutions, LLC
45 Benefit Street
Providence, RI 02909

Address Service Requested

AVOID FORECLOSURE
Don't Wait until it's Too Late – CALL NOW!
(401) 555-4663 or (877) 555-4661

WE BUY HOUSES!
Final Notice!

- Need Cash Fast?
- Need to Sell Immediately?
- Need Time to Move?

WE HAVE OPTIONS!

P.S. Rarely do problems just go away.
Visit our website below to get your FREE report:
"How to sell your house for cash in 7 days"

CALL NOW!
While you still have TIME.
401-555-4663 or 877-555-4661

www.abcREsolutions.com

To get the forms discussed in this book and an additional free gift, visit www.fastcashforms.com

Stop Your Upcoming Foreclosure In Nine Days Or Less…
Don't Let the Bank Take Your Property!

Name
Address
City, State

Dear Friend,

You can stop your Foreclosure in nine days or less by selling your house for **CASH** using a program that can possibly create equity.

We will pay you cash for your house at fair market value, not a distressed foreclosure price. If you do nothing, hoping for a miracle, the law will sell your house at Public Auction, meaning your house could be sold for 25 to 50 percent below value. Don't allow this to happen!!!

This is a money solution that will allow you to rebuild your future, but you must act now. **<u>Time is your worst enemy: Don't be embarrassed or humiliated by a lender who cares nothing about your problems.</u>**

We've been in a similar situation as yours, yet at that time, nobody lent us a helping hand. We want to provide you with that helping hand by supplying you with **KNOWLEDGE, CASH, AND OUR ABILITY TO KEEP YOUR CREDITORS FROM ANNOYING YOU!**

What Will We Do When You Call Us At 401-789-XXXX?

- David will answer the phone and ask you several questions about your home in order to start an evaluation.
- We will set up a time to visit you at your home to discuss our proposal. Our services are **FREE**. You incur **no** cost. Not everyone qualifies for our program, though we are very flexible.
- We can communicate with your lender. They will deal directly with us, as we have the cash to handle past due payments.

To get the forms discussed in this book and an additional free gift, visit www.fastcashforms.com

This can be done in one visit, but you must call us to begin this process. **Ask for Craig at 401-789-XXXX day or night.** If we are out, leave us a message.

You Can Walk Away Free and Clear

With Cash and a Fresh Start

We feel that most people may be skeptical for one major reason: They have been given empty promises in the past. This is why we offer a written guarantee

*If You Receive a Better Written Offer That is More Beneficial Than Our Proposal,
We Will Cancel Our Agreement,
Regardless of How Far Along We Are in the Process*

So you be the judge. If you call us you can't lose. If you do not, your indecision may cost you thousands of dollars if your property is sold at auction.

Make this a **TURNING POINT** in your life. **Just reach for the phone and dial 877-555-XXXX, toll free. Ask for Craig or Don. We can help!!**

To get the forms discussed in this book and an additional free gift, visit www.fastcashforms.com

With kindest regards,

Craig Picard

P.S. When you call us, rest assured that you will be under no obligation -- and you can have your foreclosure problem solved in nine days or less!

Are You Drowning In A Sea Of Debt?

«AddressBlock»

«GreetingLine»

    Don't lose hope…help is on the way! Do you think cash for your house in 10 days could help your situation? We've helped others in similar cases, proving that even in the toughest times, there is always at least one smart solution.

    As I've mentioned in prior letters to you, I'm a foreclosure specialist who searches the marketplace for homes to purchase at **fair value**—not at auction, foreclosure prices.

Here's what's in it for you:
- ✓ I will evaluate your property to determine your income potential.
- ✓ I communicate directly with your lender, and in many cases can postpone your foreclosure sale to allow us time to discuss a fair transaction. My standard procedure is to work not only quickly, but in a way that is fair to you, my customer! I don't benefit unless you receive cash. I can prevent your lender from the insistent harassment that happens during the foreclosure process.
- ✓ My specialty is helping people who are loaded down with debt.

To get the forms discussed in this book and an additional free gift, visit www.fastcashforms.com

It's human nature to be skeptical, but I believe that **the only good transactions are ones that** produce win/win solutions; n Not the kind that take advantage of people in distress.

You are in a dangerous period. Time is your worst enemy right now. Waiting will lessen your options, and my chances of helping you. Do not let fear and anxiety keep you from making a decision. Pick up the phone and call me at 401-555-XXXX.

Even if you've owned your property for only a short period, your equity could be greater than you think. But you must start the communication process by calling me immediately. My private number is 1-800-555-xxxx. We are not hard-sell artists, but real people who understand that misfortune happens to everyone (we've been there). Make this the turning point in your life, and remember that the past does not equal the future! Let me know you how to get a fresh start, with cash in your pocket in 10 days or less.

My guarantee to you:
If you get a better written offer, more beneficial than our proposal, I will cancel our contract, even if I've already begun my evaluation process.

Your lender is worried only about its money, and not about your well being! Cash is your strongest solution, and it is closer than you think. Put this all behind you. Call me at 401-555-XXXX NOW! Survival is the bottom line!

Sincerely,

Craig Picard

P.S. Let me help you by providing quick cash, and providing you with a reasonable time to move. Think of the satisfaction and confidence you'll have from taking action and getting control of the situation today!

To get the forms discussed in this book and an additional free gift, visit www.fastcashforms.com

Who Else wants to Hear Their
<u>Options</u> that the Bank didn't tell them about?

Name
Address
State Zip

Dear Name,

My name is Craig Picard. I am an individual who specializes in stopping foreclosure proceedings against homes. There are many individuals who have been told to sell the home through a realtor, and although this is an alternative, many times the owner will lose the home.

Foreclosure is a drastically unfair method used by lenders and mortgage companies to completely collect on their outstanding loans. The property is taken away from the owner and sold at a public auction. The proceeds from this sale are used to pay off the mortgage which is in default; this also includes foreclosure costs, attorney fees, and other court costs. The only thing you receive from this procedure is a black mark on your credit, possibly stopping you from ever owning a home again. This is why I spend much of my time and effort helping people avoid the damage caused by foreclosure.

I can protect your credit by stopping this foreclosure instantly.

There are a lot of possibilities which could save you from the foreclosure that don't involve selling the property. Nobody has to go through foreclosure. If I can be of service to you in your present situation, please don't hesitate to call. If I can help you over the phone, then my advice is free. Please remember that foreclosure is not the only alternative available to you.

You can reach me at 401-555-XXXX or toll free at 877-555-XXXX

Sincerely,

Craig Picard
P.S. To Find out what your options are and how we can help, CALL NOW! 401-555-XXXX or toll free at 877-555-XXXX!

To get the forms discussed in this book and an additional free gift, visit www.fastcashforms.com

STOP YOUR FORECLOSURE NOW!

«AddressBlock»

«GreetingLine»

You can **STOP** your **foreclosure** in 10 days, by instead selling your house for **cash**, using a program that can possibly create equity.

I introduced myself in a previous letter. I can pay cash at a **fair market value**, not at a distressed foreclosure price. If you do nothing—hoping for a miracle—the law will sell your house at a Public **Auction**, meaning your house could be sold for 25% to 50% below value. Don't allow this to happen!

There is a money solution that can allow you to rebuild your future, but you must act now. **Time is your worst enemy: Don't be embarrassed or humiliated by a lender who cares nothing about your situation.**

I've been in a similar situation, yet nobody lent a helping hand. I want to provide you that helping hand by supplying **knowledge, cash, and my ability to keep your creditors from annoying you further!**

When you call my local, direct line at 401-555-xxxx or toll free 1-800-555-xxxx, this is
what we'll do:
1. I will ask you several questions about your home, to evaluate your income potential
2. I will need to set up a time to visit your home to discuss my proposal.
3. I can communicate with your lender. They will deal directly with me. I have the
cash to handle past-due payments.

To get the forms discussed in this book and an additional free gift, visit www.fastcashforms.com

This can be done in our visit, but you must call me to begin the communication process. Ask for Craig Picard at 401-555-xxxx or toll free 1-800-555-xxxx, day or night. If I am out, just leave a message on my private voice mail.

You can walk away free and clear, with cash for a fresh start.

I feel most people are skeptical for one major reason. They have been given empty promises in the past. This is why I offer a **written guarantee:**

        If you get a better written offer—more beneficial than my proposal—
        I will cancel our contract, even if I've already begun my evaluation process.

You be the judge, How can you lose? Your indecision may cost you thousands of dollars when your property is sold at Public Auction. Make this a **turning point** in your life. Just reach for the phone and call 401-555-xxxx or toll free 1-800-555-xxxx. **I can help!**

Warmly,

Craig Picard

P.S. When you call me, rest assured you are under no obligation, and you won't get a hard sell! You can have cash in 10 days.

To get the forms discussed in this book and an additional free gift, visit www.fastcashforms.com

Continue to send the letters and repeat this process until one of the following happens:

1. Homeowner calls you
2. You get the letter back undeliverable
3. Auction occurs

Set up your system according to your time frame. When you put together your system, you should be printing the letters using the mail merge feature of the word processing software you are using. The mail merge will automatically insert the homeowners name into the letter. This technique will increase your response rate by over 25%. When you print the letters out, save some time and print not only the first letter you will send out but also at least the next four letters.

This will save you a lot of time since the letters can be stuffed and ready to go. Another method is to save the mail merger letters in a file on the computer and label the date it needs to be placed in the mail. If you know how many days it will take to stuff, stamp and address the letters, then you can back into the date you need to print the letters.

Response Enhancers

- Mail merge the recipient's name into the Letter
- Colored paper (goldenrod or light gray)
- Square envelope
- Lumpy mail
- Teaser
    - Fake check in the envelope
    - Offer in the envelope

To get the forms discussed in this book and an additional free gift, visit www.fastcashforms.com

Delegate or Outsource

Now that you have created a system for your direct mail marketing, you need to delegate it to someone else in your company or you need to outsource the function to another company that specializes in that field. You may want to do it yourself at first so that you understand the system and how long it takes.

Building a system also makes it easier for you to train someone. Document the steps and create a manual for someone to follow. Delegating will free up time for you to make more offers and talk to more homeowners. Your goal should be to delegate this as soon as possible.

Who will do this Job?

Anyone who has legible handwriting can do this job. Remember the most important step here is that the envelope is hand addressed. You can ask friends, family, your children, your mom, niece, nephew, or babysitter. Maybe there is a high school student in your neighborhood or circle of friends. Besides the penmanship, they also need to be reliable, trustworthy and responsible.

You can check with Senior Centers in your area and post a flyer. Try an assisted living facility since most of the people that live there are looking for things to keep them busy. They are also probably on a fixed income and the extra money will go a long way. I have had success using the local Veterans Administration. They have at least one in every state. They pretty much have a coordinator that works with small businesses like ours to do piece work. They are efficient as well, as I have dropped off 1,000 piece mailings and have gotten them back in 24-48 hours.

You can also post an advertisement on www.craigslist.com under the category "domestic gigs". A local mailing service might also provide you with the service but make sure that they will be able to

To get the forms discussed in this book and an additional free gift, visit www.fastcashforms.com

hand address the envelopes. Finally you will need to supply the people with the necessary items such as lists, envelopes, letters, return address labels, stamps, sponge and pens. Have them sign your name to the letter.

The homeowner doesn't know what your signature looks like anyway. You might be wondering about the return address label mentioned above. You are not supposed to use any labels but in an attempt to make the envelope more personable, you can order return address labels that have balloons on it or a cat or dog or just something plain and simple like you might get on a letter from a friend. It just really makes the envelope stand out from the other mail.

Make sure the label is white with black writing and the balloons or whatever are in color. When addressing the envelope and signing the letter, make sure you use blue ink as well. Blue ink just stands out more and typical junk mail uses black ink.

Returned Letters

You will be surprised by the amount of letters that come back to you as undeliverable, return to sender or forwarding order has expired but these will be some of your biggest money makers. They have vacated the property and detached themselves from the property. Your biggest hurdle has already been removed. They have already put the solution behind them and started over.

There is no particular reason why they leave the house. In some cases they see the writing on the wall and make a decision to leave and start over. In other cases it may have been a job relocation and they were unable to sell. Perhaps it was a divorce and neither spouse wanted to stay. You will quickly learn it doesn't matter why people leave a house with equity and let it go vacant. They just do. Although you just removed the hurdle of the owner leaving the house,

To get the forms discussed in this book and an additional free gift, visit www.fastcashforms.com

in your mind an even larger problem has popped up. Where do I go and how do I find them?

Finding the Owner

There are several things you can do to try to locate the owner. Send a post card to the vacant house but make sure to put "address service requested" on the front of the post card under your return address. This tells the post office to send you any known address for the homeowner. If they have one, you will get a message from the post office in your mail box telling you they have an address and there is a small fee (under a dollar) to get it.

You can now continue to direct mail to them. If the address is local, you should stop by and knock on the door. Also try to find a phone number for them now that you have the address. The next place to look will be the neighbors surrounding the house. Typically the neighbors know what was going on and where they went. If the neighbor doesn't know be sure to give them one of your business cards. Tell them you will pay them $500 or $1,000 referral fee if they provide you information that leads you to buy the property. The neighbor may see the homeowner return to gather mail or other belongings they left behind.

Be sure to knock on all the neighbor's doors that surround the property. Don't stop at one. The next step is to order a skip trace. There are many companies out there that provide the service and they will cost anywhere from $10-$50 per search and most only charge if they can secure an address for you.

Communicating with Owner

Once you find the homeowner that vacated the property, you have jumped over one hurdle but have approached another. They have separated themselves from the house and have moved on. They really

To get the forms discussed in this book and an additional free gift, visit www.fastcashforms.com

don't care what you have to offer. You might think if you offer them money, why wouldn't they take it? It really depends upon the situation. Your job is to convince them that they can walk away with money and make it as easy as possible for them.

They walked away because they were in great pain so make sure that you make this as easy and the least time consuming as possible. Once you gain their trust and demonstrate to them what is in it to them, they will typically sign the deed and leave you with everything.

Follow up   Follow up   Follow up

The most important part of marketing is the follow up. I can't emphasize this enough. Make sure you return all calls promptly. If you let even an hour go by, you may loose the deal. You must continue to follow up until they sell, die, or have fixed their situation. Stay in touch with them periodically even when their situation has been fixed because chances are that at some point in the future they will fall back into the same situation and will need your help. Most of the business that you do will be done after the fourth follow up. Most people only follow up twice.

This is what separates us from our competition. Put a system together for follow up. You can use something like ACT or Goldmine. These are database programs that will provide you with a list of who to follow up with each day and who to schedule future follow up with. You can even document the details of your contact with them whether is it manual or electronic, you must have a system.

To get the forms discussed in this book and an additional free gift, visit www.fastcashforms.com

Chapter 4: Relationship Marketing

If you haven't heard it by now let me be the first to alert you, to be a successful real estate investor, you don't need to be in the real estate business, you need to be in the Relationship Business. One of the best things about the relationship business is it's a FREE method of marketing. The key is you need to be out there networking and meeting people to build your relationships.

One of the most important players in the Real Estate Business that you should be targeting and developing a relationship with are Real Estate Agents/Brokers. They have direct access to people looking to sell their property and they have access to the Multiple Listing Service (MLS). The multiple listing service is a database and software that is used by real estate brokers representing sellers who they have a listing contract with. They are able to use the MLS to share information about their listing with other brokers who may represent potential buyers or wish to cooperate with a seller's broker in finding a buyer for the property or asset.

As you can imagine the MLS, or multiple listing service, can prove to be a wealth of information. When you develop a relationship with a realtor they will share the information with you. Keep in mind that there are a lot of listings on the MLS but they are not all <u>motivated</u> sellers and as we mentioned earlier; the only type of seller we want to work with is a motivated seller. In the next section we are going to discuss how to identify who the motivated sellers are.

Keyword Searches on the MLS

When working with a realtor to utilize the MLS, it is a good idea to ask them to look on a weekly basis as new properties appear. This will give you the best chances for identifying properties quickly as

To get the forms discussed in this book and an additional free gift, visit www.fastcashforms.com

they are listed and before anyone else has a chance to put them under agreement.

The first step in locating properties that may be of interest to you is to narrow down the search area. If you are near a larger metropolitan area then you may need to narrow the search criteria down even further to a specific neighborhood, especially if a number of new listings are coming onto the MLS each week. When choosing the neighborhoods to consider for your search parameters, consider where most of the entry level homes are where first time home buyers are going to buy. In most cases that is going to be in the lower-income neighborhoods.

To identify the potential motivated sellers we want to target, you can also use a variety of different keywords as search criteria in order to bring up a listing of properties that are likely to match what you are looking for. It is even possible that your real estate agent may not be aware of what to look for. Understanding the specific keywords to target when looking through the online database can go a long way toward helping to identify the correct properties as quickly as possible. Ask the realtor that you are working with to send you email alerts anytime new properties that meet your criteria come up on the MLS so that you will have the best chance possible of taking early action on these properties.

Such keywords include the following:
- Vacant
- Needs TLC
- Handyman Special
- Needs Rehab
- Estate Sale
- Probate
- Needs Work

To get the forms discussed in this book and an additional free gift, visit www.fastcashforms.com

- As-Is
- Corporate owned
- Bank owned
- Foreclosure

Days on the Market

It is also helpful to understand that the number of days the property has been on the market can also be an important factor to consider as well. This is because the longer that a property has been on the market, the more likely it is that the seller will be desperate to sell it. You should also pay specific attention to properties that have been on the market for a long time and are also in poor condition. There is nothing worse for a seller than a property that has two strikes against it. These are properties that the seller is going to be more motivated to get rid of quickly as well because they are hard to sell.

What is the Most Important Info on the Listing Sheet?

The listing sheet can be a critical piece of information when determining which properties will provide the best prospects. You must know which information on the listing sheet is the most important and should be given proper consideration.
Your real estate agent will provide you with the listing sheet, which provides a summary of information regarding each property. In most cases the listing sheet will be a single sheet for each property. This sheet will usually contain the following information:
- Property address
- Listed asking price
- Type of property-single family home, condo or townhouse
- Number of bedrooms
- Number of bathrooms
- Number of days the property has been on the market

To get the forms discussed in this book and an additional free gift, visit www.fastcashforms.com

- A description of the property

Generally, the description of the property will not be very detailed, but it will include information about the current condition of the property as well as any other relevant facts. It is extremely important to pay attention to this information because it can provide critical details regarding whether the seller might have motivation to sell the property at a discounted price.

Besides the number of days that the property has been on the market, there are also several other critical clues that can give you an idea of whether the bank may be motivated to sell at a discount. Look for phrases such as the following:

- "Bring all offers!"
- "Motivated Seller"
- "Owner says sell!"
- "Foreclosure property!"
- "Just needs a little TLC"
- "Great property for a handy-man!"

When you see phrases like these that indicate the owner, which is the bank, is anxious to sell and/or that the property is in need of repairs, this is a good indication that the bank is ready to get rid of the property and will take whatever they can get.

Which Agents to Work With

There is certainly not lack of real estate agents available. The real estate industry can be quite lucrative. As a result, there are numerous professionals in that industry. That does not mean that you should work with just anyone; however. It is critical that you make the

To get the forms discussed in this book and an additional free gift, visit www.fastcashforms.com

time and the effort to choose a real estate agent to work with that you can trust and who also has the experience that you need.

Rather than simply working with the first real estate agent that comes along, it is a good idea to speak with several in order to find the best agent that will meet your needs. At a minimum, you should speak with three agents before making a decision. Try to focus on those agents who have some experience in the industry and when possible, those agents who specifically have experience with Bank owned properties, aka Bank REO's (Real Estate Owner).

The reason you want the Realtor to have experience with REO's is because they are one of the **most motivated** sellers on the MLS. One of your marketing strategies should be focusing on building relationships with REO agents. Developing the relationship will enable you to score some bank owned properties. Most banks don't typically sell directly to investors. They usually solicit three realtors to get price opinions and then list the property through one of them and this is how they dispose of their real estate assets so agents are typically the quickest way to get your deals.

Questions to Ask When Interviewing a Agent

When interviewing potential agents that you are considering working with, there are several questions that you should make sure that you ask in order to gain an idea of their experience and how well you will work together.

Have you worked with investors in the past?

While you should not necessarily rule out agents who have never worked with investors in the past, if you do decide to work with someone who does not have this kind of experience, you will need to

To get the forms discussed in this book and an additional free gift, visit www.fastcashforms.com

make sure they fully understand your position. Most real estate agents are accustomed to working with clients who are looking to purchase a single family residence in which they will live. As a result, there is no need to consider the profit potential of the property.

That, of course, is not the case, when you are looking to purchase investment property and you need to make sure that the agent understands this. An agent who has worked with investors in the past will have a far better understanding of what you are looking for and will also understand that you will need to focus on finding properties that will be able to sell quickly.

The agent should be aware that you will expect them to identify properties that are in desirable neighborhoods and also to warn you regarding any properties that might not sell as quickly.

You should also advise the agent that you prefer for them to provide you only with market values that are conservative and fair. Too many times, the market value of a property can be hyped and that does not benefit anyone. Remember that in order to make a profit on a REO, it is essential that you not overpay for the property.

Ultimately, the agent should understand that his or her ability to identify properties which you will be able to buy at a discount will help them to earn a much easier commission in the long run because it will allow you to in turn offer the property to prospective buyer at a price that under market value.

How much experience do you have in the real estate industry?

You should view the number of years that an agent has worked in the industry somewhat objectively. Certainly, an agent that has worked in the industry for several years will have more experience, but keep in mind that even an agent that does not have as much experience may be able to make up for that lack of experience with enthusiasm. It is sometimes the case that an agent who has quite a bit of experience will simply not have the drive or the hunger that you need.

How much time are you willing to spend with me to meet my goals?

Time is money in every industry and that is true of the real estate industry as well. You should be absolutely clear with any agents that you consider working with what you expect, especially in terms of them searching the MLS weekly and researching fair market values of properties. It should be made clear to the agent that in exchange for their time spent they are likely to gain a profitable payoff in terms of your purchasing multiple properties each year. Consequently, the agent stands to gain several good commissions per year.

Keep in mind that ultimately, you need to focus on identifying the agent who is willing to dedicate the time necessary to help you achieve your goals and who will also promptly respond to your needs.

How to Get an Agent to Work with you if you are New

One problem that you may run into if you are new to the field of real estate investing is that some agents may be hesitant to work with you. This is especially true if it is an agent who is quite experienced and therefore has a number of clients demanding their services. It only stands to reason, when you look at it from the perspective of the real estate agent that they would not want to expend a significant amount of time tracking down properties when they cannot be absolutely certain that you will indeed purchase properties, leading to commissions for them.

To get the forms discussed in this book and an additional free gift, visit www.fastcashforms.com

It is imperative that you be able to convince a real estate agent that you are indeed serious about this venture and furthermore that you have the financial ability to do so.

One method that you might consider is to go ahead and obtain a letter from a bank indicating that you are pre-approved for a loan up to a certain amount in the event that you find a property that suits your needs. This would certainly indicate to the agent that you have the financial resources available to you to purchase a property when they locate one for you.

You might also consider writing a check out to the local escrow company for a small percentage of a prospective purchase price and having the agent hold onto that check until a property is located and it can then be put toward the required escrow amount. This would also demonstrate your seriousness as well as your financial ability to proceed with a purchase.

REALTOR RELATIONSIPS – DEAL FAST TRACK

Two of the biggest mistakes I see investors make is that they don't build relationships with the right agents and they don't do anything to differentiate themselves from the competition. The tips and techniques we share with you below will put you on the Fast Track to getting your first deal through realtor relationships and cashing your next check.

Listing Agents: To streamline your success and get deals more quickly, work with agents that get a lot of their own listings. There are a few reasons why it will streamline your success. First of all you will have a direct link between you and the seller so the agent will know the sellers motivations and situation. Second, if they have a deal that is already under contract and the deal falls through, you have the possibility of them calling you to buy the deal. Third, if you are

To get the forms discussed in this book and an additional free gift, visit www.fastcashforms.com

competing against another buyer that has a buyer's agent representing them, your agent is going to encourage the seller to take your offer rather than the other buyers since they won't have to split the commission if you get the deal.

One of the most important reasons is so you can get access to pocket listings which are listings that are shown to buyers before the agent lists the property on the MLS. . This is how it works. (Note: You won't get these at first since you haven't formed a relationship with the agent but you will as time goes on if you use our techniques.)

Work with Multiple Agents: Never sign and Exclusive relationship agreement with a realtor. An exclusive agreement will only allow you to work with that one agent and in some agreements they will get to make a commission even when you find your own deals through your own marketing. This will slow down your success and reduce your profits. You want to be working with multiple agents so you have several agents you can get pocket listings from.

CASH is King: When you contact agents you are going to tell them how you are investor looking to purchase properties, update them, and resell them to retail buyers. One key thing you want to mention is that you will be buying the properties CASH. Now, don't get scared if you don't have the cash. You never told the realtor is was going to be your cash. You can use your equity line, Hard Money, Private Money, or your Cash Buyers money if wholesaling. The key is to let them know cash because then you can close quickly and don't have to get financing through the banks. When buying properties cash, you will be a great candidate to buy their listings where they have a **Motivated Seller**.

Proof of Funds: Proof of funds are a document that demonstrates that a person has the funds available to use for a

To get the forms discussed in this book and an additional free gift, visit www.fastcashforms.com

transaction. It usually comes in the form of a statement of an account like a bank account or brokerage account. The purpose of the document is to ensure that the funds required for the transaction are obtainable. If you are afraid of personal info from a bank statement getting into the wrong hands, black out the account number and any other info you don't want them to see.

Although using your account is best, proof of funds can be something other than cash in your bank account, such as a friends or family members account, a potential partners account or even one of your cash buyers accounts. It is not required that you actually use the funds in the specific account you show to fund the deal. You may show the proof of funds from one account up front and then close the deal using a different source. You can also use an approval letter from a bank or private/hard money lender as well as cash. Lastly you can use the resource we gave you as part of this program, www.rewealthfunding.com which is just a click away.

Breakfast or Lunch: Get to know them. More importantly get them to know you so that they can bring you into deals before they alert other investors. If you fail to have a meaningful face to face meeting with them, you will fail to get the deals you are looking for. Remember, this is a relationship business and you need to develop a personal relationship with people.

Follow-up, Follow-up, Follow-up: I'm not sure how many times you have heard this but we are going to say it again. The deal is in the Follow-up. How can you build a relationship with someone unless you are following up on a regular basis. You need to be following up with agents at least once every 7-10 days. You are not going to be just calling them every 7-10 days asking for deals. You need to be following up by giving them feedback on deals they send you so you don't leave them hanging.

You can train them so you don't waste their time and yours in the future on deals you are not interested in. Also, follow up by

To get the forms discussed in this book and an additional free gift, visit www.fastcashforms.com

sending them something so you will increase the number of touches with them. Have you ever heard of the law of reciprocity, when someone receives something, feel like they need to give back to that person. In this case, it would be the agent sending you a good deal. Send them information on the Real Estate market or something they might be able to share with their other clients. Send them a thank you card or a gift card to Dunkin Donuts or Starbucks thanking them for their time.

    Again, your goal here is to building a personal relationship with them and have as many touches with them as possible so we are constantly on their mind. Most other investors fail at this so follow these steps and you will have success.

To get the forms discussed in this book and an additional free gift, visit www.fastcashforms.com

Chapter 5: Pre-Screening Deals

If you are marketing correctly, your phone will begin to ring and you need to be prepared to answer it. When you are first starting out, you will want to answer the calls yourself. However this will not be the best use of your time. You want to spend your time making calls and working on your business. You typically will not buy a house or counsel a person in foreclosure over the phone so why should you be answering it.

When the phone rings, there are certain questions the homeowner must answer before you can determine if you can help them out and which method will be right for them. So now that we know that you don't want to be answering the phone, who will it be? You have a few options here:

> Answering machine/voice mail
> Answering Service
> Websites

Answering Machine/ Voicemail

This is the least preferred method. When people in foreclosure decide to call, they want to speak to a live person. They want the help that the letter said they would get. When they get a voice mail or answering machine, most will hang up. When they hang up, they are calling the next person who sent them a letter. You will lose two thirds of your calls if you allow them to go to voice mail.

Why should they leave you a message, you are not going to call back anyway. It is amazing how many voice mail messages are not returned.

To get the forms discussed in this book and an additional free gift, visit www.fastcashforms.com

People don't like voice mail and don't trust it. They want a live person to talk to, not a machine especially the extremely motivated owners. They want to get a solution to their problem immediately. If you cannot afford to pay someone to answer your phone or an answering service, you can allow calls to go to you as a last resort. If you are going to do this make sure that all your marketing phone numbers go to your cell phone. If possible, route all your calls through an 800 number or toll free number so you can capture their phone number.

Answering Service

If you have not yet quit your day job and are doing real estate investing part time, you may not have the ability to answer the phone. The next best thing to you will be a live voice. Remember they don't know who will answer the phone. In the busy world we live in today, we don't expect to reach the person but I am sure glad when I get a live voice. When you are unavailable, transfer all your marketing phone lines to the answering service. I wish that was all you had to do but there are several more steps involved. Anytime you are not the one answering the phone or have delegated any function, you need to first train, then trust, but verify.

Why would you need to train an answering service? Don't they already know what to do? The answer is that some will and some won't. I always go under the assumption that they won't. When you call the answering service for the first time, you must interview them to see if they are a fit for your business. Some will just take messages and others will go through a script and get answers to questions. You want the one that will ask questions and go through a script.

To get the forms discussed in this book and an additional free gift, visit www.fastcashforms.com

Now that they know what to say when the phone rings, will they answer it when it rings? How many rings will it take? You want your phone answered within four rings. Most people will hang up after four rings. The next thing to evaluate is what happens after they answer the phone. Do they get to speak with someone or do they get put on hold? Putting your client on hold is alright, however, if they are on hold for more that 20 seconds, they will start to hang up and call your competition.

If they do put callers on hold, make sure that they have on hold music because callers are more likely to stay on hold when there is music versus silence. At least with the on hold music they know they have not been disconnected. When the phone is finally taken off hold, they must be kind and friendly as they interact with the prospect.

How will you know if your answering service is doing what they are supposed to? You must call into your answering service from a number that they don't know. Pretend you are a customer and see what they do. When you first start out with an answering service, you will need to do this once a day and after you feel more comfortable; you can switch to a weekly checkup. In order to locate an answering service, you can look in your local phone book; ask other investors at your local REIA or do an internet search.

Rates vary widely but you can expect to pay at least $80 per month and a per minute charge in addition to that. You need to shop around and find the best price for the best service.

Assistant

If you have an assistant, you will want to train them to answer the incoming calls. You can use the incoming call script to train them on what to say. Take the first few calls with them so they can hear how

To get the forms discussed in this book and an additional free gift, visit www.fastcashforms.com

you answer the phone and transition into questions. Train them on how to recognize motivation because you want to know about those opportunities as soon as possible. Make sure they tell all callers that someone will call them back within 30 minutes.

Most people will wait the 30 minutes since you will be calling with solutions to their problems. Try to call the motivated ones back immediately or within ten minutes. The more your assistant is able to answer the phone between doing other tasks, the more time you will have to find more opportunities. Efficiency is the key to this business. Form a system for repetitive tasks and train others to complete these tasks or jobs and you will be free to grow your business.

Use Websites to Pre-Screen

n the business world today websites are a must. If you don't have a website, people will not trust you. Besides building credibility and describing your company's services, your website is a great place to pre-screen leads. Your website should be on every piece of marketing material that you send out. The great thing about the World Wide Web is that it is available 24 hours per day seven days a week. When you are sleeping it is working for you.

We have had many sellers contact us through our website rather than calling us. Some people are afraid of the phone or are not sure what will happen when they call. Others are unable to deal with their problems during the day and spend many sleepless nights searching the internet for a solution. Make sure that your website has a qualifying page that has the same sort of qualifying questions that the incoming call script has. The qualifying page is where you will direct them to go so they won't end up at your main page and be lost and confused. If your site provides an easy way for them to leave their contact information you will have success.

To get the forms discussed in this book and an additional free gift, visit www.fastcashforms.com

Keep your qualifying page as short as possible. I know you want to know everything about them but they may not want to take the time to fill it out. Get the essential details that you need on the website and when you speak to them live, you can get the rest of your questions answered.

Incoming Call Script

Prescreening your leads is essential in the Quick Turn business. You can't go see every property that you receive a call on. You will waste a lot of time and end up spinning your wheels. WE have provided you with an incoming call script designed to determine how motivated the seller is and if it is worth going to see the property. You will need to ask the right questions to determine what solutions you can provide them.

Before you go into the script it is important to understand what we are looking for. The most important thing we are looking for is motivation. If they are motivated when they respond, you have a chance at helping them. If they are unmotivated, you are not going to be able to effectively provide assistance. It is one thing for the owner to be depressed or upset about their situation, but it is another to be unmotivated.

When I first started taking calls, I used to spend five or ten minutes per call and sometimes more. I spent too much time listening to their situation rather than asking them questions that would help me to determine what solutions I could offer. Using the incoming call script in this chapter will help you to get the information you need in a timely manner. In most cases you should be able to get the information you need, and determine what the next step is going to be within five minutes. In order to get the most out of the script, we will provide detail on each question and the purpose of asking it.

To get the forms discussed in this book and an additional free gift, visit www.fastcashforms.com

INCOMING CALL SCRIPT

Good (Morning, Afternoon, Evening) Creative Foreclosure Solutions, How can I help you?

Yes, I'm calling about….

Thanks for calling. Could you tell me how you heard about us? *(if letter)* Ok.. Could you please read me the headline of the letter?

I'm sorry, my name is _____ what's your name *(FIRST, LAST)*?

(Say first name) could I get your number there just in case we get disconnected?

CELL: **HOME:**   **WORK:**
EMAIL:

What is the address of the property?

I need to ask you some questions to see how we can help you.

Are you the property owner?

How long have you owned the property?

Can you tell me a little bit about your situation *(show empathy)*?

When is the auction date **(foreclosure)?**
What have you done so far to stop foreclosure **(foreclosure)**?

Can you tell me a little about the property?
What is the condition of the property? Does it need any major repairs?

How much do you think the property is worth?
How did you come up with that value?

How many mortgages do you have on the property?   Are you Behind?

To get the forms discussed in this book and an additional free gift, visit www.fastcashforms.com

When is the last time the mortgage company accepted a payment **(foreclosure)**?

How much do you need to make up the back payments and bring the loan current **(foreclosure)**?

Have you considered selling the property **(foreclosure)**?

If we could offer you cash and close quickly, What's the least amount of money you would accept for the property **(most important Question)?**

I would like to come see your property. What would be better time to come over? Today at 3pm or tonight at 7pm?

To get the forms discussed in this book and an additional free gift, visit www.fastcashforms.com

INCOMING CALL SCRIPT WALK THRU

Good (morning, afternoon, evening) <u>insert company name</u> ; how can I help you?
You want the greeting to be as professional as possible. Many people are afraid to call. With a warm greeting they will be open to sharing information. Use your company name, especially if it has solutions in the name. They are looking for solutions and you are a solutions provider.

Thanks for calling. Can you tell me how you heard about my company?
Of all the questions you will ask, this is probably the most important. The answer to this question will make you or save you money in the future regardless of what happens to the person who is calling. Use the answer to this question to track your marketing. If they say letter, ask them to read you the headline. Keep in mind that they may have already told you the way they found you when they first introduced themselves. There's no need to ask them twice so make sure you pay attention to what they say and make sure you record their answer.

I'm sorry; my name is <u>insert your name</u>. What's yours?
You are probably thinking what I am sorry for. Sorry you don't know their name. Sorry you didn't introduce yourself sooner. Sorry you forgot the name they told you 20 seconds ago. It is just an easier way to ask their name. You don't want to sound robotic like you are interviewing them.

(Insert their first name), could I get your number there in case we get disconnected?
This is where most real estate investors make a mistake. They assume that the number on the called ID is the number where they can be reached. Always ask this question. Then ask for their cell phone

To get the forms discussed in this book and an additional free gift, visit www.fastcashforms.com

number. After they provide their cell phone number, ask for their work number. If they don't want to provide that, later in the conversation find out where they work or ask them what is the best number to reach you at. You can't have enough ways to contact them. When I first started, I never asked for a second or third number until on two separate occasions I had called back and a homeowner and the number were disconnected.

Now, I try to get three phone numbers because when people get behind on their mortgage, they are usually behind on everything else as well and it is only a matter of time before all their numbers will be disconnected and you will have no way of reaching them. A hot lead will turn into a cold one. Sure you might be able to hunt them down but that could take hours of your time where asking for the number up front only takes a few seconds.

What is the address of the property?
You would think this one doesn't need any explanation but without the address you can't do anything. When I don't use the script, this is always the item I forget to ask.

Are you the property owner?
You need to know who you are dealing with. If they are not the owner, you need to find out who is because only the owner can ultimately make a decision. If they are the owner, ask if there are any other owners.

How long have you owned the property?
The answers to this question will probably not tell you anything immediately, but it may help you later. If they say they just bought it within the past two years, they may not have much equity depending on

To get the forms discussed in this book and an additional free gift, visit www.fastcashforms.com

the phase of the market your area is in. If they have owned it forever, they may have a lot of equity and your strategy might change.

When is the auction date(foreclosure only)?
Many homeowners will not know this or you may have to ask them another way to get the answer. Tell them to look on the letter they got from the bank's attorney. This piece of information will tell you how quickly you need to act. They may say it is tomorrow and in most cases we can't help them with less than 48 hours prior to the auction because we won't have enough information to assess our risk. If they have enough time, you will now know your timeline to react.

What have you done so far to stop foreclosure?
The homeowner may need a thought jogger on this one. Basically you want to know, have they tried to sell the property, have they tried to refinance, have they tried to work something out with their current lender. The answer to this question will help you determine what your next step is going to be. If they say you are the first one that they called, you can use the full solutions approach. Maybe they have tried to refinance but have been denied.

    I will then ask them if they have considered selling. I will also ask if they know anyone who could lend them the money to make up the back payments. If they say they want to keep the house, I will ask them if we found a way to make up your back payments, would you be able to pay the monthly payment on time every month. I also ask what has changed in their situation since missing a mortgage payment. If their situation hasn't changed most likely they will not be able to afford the monthly payments even if we find a way to make the back payments. If this is the case then we show them that selling their house is their best option.

To get the forms discussed in this book and an additional free gift, visit www.fastcashforms.com

Can you tell me a little bit about your situation?
This is a motivational question. How they answer this question will tell you how motivated they are. If they tell you that they are selling because right down the street, Joey down the street just got "x" for his property and they want to see what they can get for theirs, most likely they are not motivated. If they say, both of my parents recently passed, I live out of state, the property is out dated and I don't have time to deal with it, then most likely they are extremely motivated. Make sure when they are telling you their situation you show empathy. You are trying to build rapport with them and some of the sellers that call might be going through a tough time. Remember, your ultimate goal is to provide a win-win situation and you are trying to help these people.

Can you tell me about the property?
You are looking for real basic information like beds, baths, and age. You will use this information to quickly determine what the property is worth. Also it helps you ask fewer questions so it doesn't make it sound like you are interviewing them. Many times while answering this question they will give you the answer to your next question without you even asking.

What is the condition of the property? Does it need major repairs?
This is a question that you want to let them talk. Let them tell you what's wrong but most of the time they will list all the recent improvements. The recent improvements list is good but you want to get a ballpark idea of how much money it will cost to repair the property. If they give you a number of how much it would take to fix the property up, it will always be too low.

What do you think the property is worth?
The answer here will help you to start to see what sort of solutions you can provide. They will provide a number or tell you they have no idea. Follow up with: *"How did you come up with that value?"* If they say

To get the forms discussed in this book and an additional free gift, visit www.fastcashforms.com

the house across the street just sold for that amount and this is newer, you now may have a "comp" or this may indicate their motivation level. You will also start to see what they are thinking in terms of value. Your question at the end will determine what they would be willing to sell for and sometimes they will sell for a lower number than they think it is worth.

How many mortgages do you have on the property? Are you behind?
This is the area you will need to gather further information about the debt on the property. You need to find this information out before you can go any further. If they don't know how many payments they are behind you can ask, *"When is the last time the mortgage company accepted a payment?"* This is just a nicer way of asking about their payment situation.

"How much do you need to make up the back payments and make the loan current?"
This is critical information as you may have to use this in your analysis when deciding to buy. Maybe you have a private lender that will lend them the money. If they give any objection as to why you need to know this, let them know that you may be able to get them a private loan but you need to get this information to see if their house qualifies.

Last Question(most important):

If we could pay you all cash and close quickly, what is the least amount of money you could accept?

You are asking them their bottom line. Asking this question could make the difference between the property being a deal and not being a deal. I've seen sellers drop $20,000+ when we have asked this question. You need to let them name a number first or else you may pay too much.

To get the forms discussed in this book and an additional free gift, visit www.fastcashforms.com

"I would like to see the property. What would be a better time to come over; today at 3pm or tonight at 7pm?"

If you ask a close ended question here, you may not like the response. By asking the question this way, they may feel those are their only choices and they need to choose one. **Nugget:** IF you are not sure if its' a deal you should still setup the appointment. It's easier to cancel an appointment then to have to call back and try to get one.

Calling the Homeowner

If you are not the person taking the calls directly, you must have a system in place to get the information as soon as possible. If you are using an answering machine or voice mail, you will want to check for messages quite often (Again this is not the best option. Remember, Live Voice if possible). If you are using an answering service, most have the capability to fax, email, or text message the information to you. If you are using an assistant to answer the phone, you will want to train them to recognize the opportunities that need your attention the fastest such as limited amount of time prior to the auction date or motivated seller who is looking for a fair price.

You need to follow up ASAP. They want a solution now and will keep calling your competition until you provide one that is a win-win. If they are looking to sell, good deals are usually gone in hours. If you don't follow up promptly, you will loose deals. Only call motivated homeowners. If they are not motivated to solve their problems, then you will have an uncooperative person that will continue to waste your time.

Some investors have a hard time making the call back to the homeowner. There are several hurdles that you must first get passed:

To get the forms discussed in this book and an additional free gift, visit www.fastcashforms.com

Fear of failure, fear of success, afraid you will sound correct, don't have time, afraid to look stupid, lazy, and procrastinator. There are a bunch of reasons not to call; however, you need to get them out of your head. Experience will be your best teacher. The good news is that the homeowner doesn't know what you are supposed to say or do and you know more than they do. If they knew what to do they wouldn't be calling so the bottom line is call them so you can see how you can help. Your goal when calling back is to get the appointment. The following are the steps when calling a homeowner back: Repeat the information that was given, get a series of positives or yes's, ask the closing question to get the appointment.

Nugget: We have found that one of the biggest fears for new investors not answering the phone or for calling the seller back is the fear of not knowing the answer to a question they might ask. First of all if the seller is motivated (the ones you should be focused on), they aren't going to ask a bunch of questions. They just want to get out of their situation.

If for some reason if a seller does ask you a question that you can't answer just tell them your partner handles that and you'll check with him/her and call them back. I've never had anyone object to this. People are just looking for help.

RETURN CALL SCRIPT

Mr. homeowner, it's (your name), from (company name) you called today and provided my assistant some information about your situation and I wanted to go over the information you provided, is now a good time to talk?

Excellent.

Repeat info given, ask if it is correct, get a series of yes's.

To get the forms discussed in this book and an additional free gift, visit www.fastcashforms.com

Is there any other information that I should know about your situation?

The next step is for me to come out and see the property. When would be a good time for me to meet with you at your house? Today at 4pm or tonight at 6pm?

By the way, will all of the people on the mortgage be available at that time? It is much better if I can explain the options directly to everyone involved at the same time.

I look forward to meeting you _____ at _____.

HOW TO DETERMINE IF YOU SHOULD YOU MEET WITH SELLER

When deciding if you should meet with the homeowner, there are two qualifiers. Do they have equity and are they motivated or at least willing to cooperate. Without these two components, you will find yourself unable to help them. If they have equity, your goal will be to meet with the seller and get the property under contract. This way you can either buy the property and sell it as a handyman special to a retail buyer (if it needs only cosmetic updates), fix it up and sell it to retail buyer or get it under agreement and wholesale it to a cash buyer.

If they have a little equity but not enough for you to buy or wholesale the property then you do have options. You might be able to buy it via Lease Option which we will talk about later or you can pass the lead to a realtor. Most investors just throw these in the trash. This is what you don't want to do. You want to be a transaction engineer and want to try to get something out of every lead that you get a call on

To get the forms discussed in this book and an additional free gift, visit www.fastcashforms.com

even if it just a referral fee or it helps you improve a relationship. If they have no equity, you will not have many options. You will have to do a short sale.

A short sale is the term to describe the lender accepting less than what is owed on the loan and marking the loan paid in full. If you have no desire to do short sales, you can consult with them over the phone to see if any of the other options might work, never throw away the lead. Remember we want to to be transaction engineers. You have a few options: (a) Get some education on the subject of short sales. (b) Find out what investors in your area do short sales and work out an arrangement with them to do the short sale. (c) **Nugget:** Many realtors are doing short sales so pass the lead to one of the realtors you are building a relationship with. If you start sending them leads, do you think they will be more inclined to send you some deals?

Realtor Lists the Property

As just mentioned, in some cases you will determine that the property has some equity but not enough for you to purchase and make a profit. If the property is in good condition or at least a condition that will allow it to be financed, a quality realtor may be a good option. You will want a realtor that lists and sells houses in the same area as the subject property. They should be one of the top realtors in the area. I usually ask them for 20% of their net commission and tell them to pay it to me as a marketing fee. Some may agree to this or they may negotiate something different.

It may take a few leads that turn into sold listings before they are truly on board with the marketing fee but most realtors I know would take any listing that has some equity in it and can be listed for under market to sell quickly. If you can't find a realtor that will give you part of their commission at first, just give realtors the listing if you

To get the forms discussed in this book and an additional free gift, visit www.fastcashforms.com

can't buy it. Like we mentioned earlier, it will help you build a relationship with them and will make them feel like they owe you something. Sometimes you need to give to get. You might as well get something out of the deal versus throwing the lead in the trash.

What if I'm a Realtor

Some investors are realtors including myself. You might be thinking, "Why would I give the listing to someone else?" "If listing with a realtor is the best option, then why shouldn't I list the property?". If you are a Realtor and in the business of quick turning real estate, you have a decision to make. Are you a Realtor or Investor? If you are an investor, then the best use of your time will be meeting with more potential sellers, not spending your valuable time meeting with prospective buyers of a property. You are an investor and should be out finding more deals to bring into your business.

Let someone else spend the time to list and show and sell the property. Yes, you are giving up on some potential income, but you only have so much time in the day and where do you have the opportunity to make more money as a Realtor or Investor? Of course, as an Investor. Now you may be a very successful Realtor and make good money as a Realtor but I would take advantage of your access to the MLS and your network of other Realtors and spend more time on finding deals and flipping them.

If you are not convinced over the next couple of months, track how many hours you spend as a Realtor and what you make per hour. Then track the number of hours you spend on a deal as an investor and calculate what you are earning per hour.

Short Sale

To get the forms discussed in this book and an additional free gift, visit www.fastcashforms.com

Some of the homeowners in foreclosure will be best suited for this option. A short sale is when you offer to buy the property for less than what is owed on the mortgage. In some cases the lender will discount the mortgage and accept a lesser amount as payment in full. Some lenders will discount and some won't. Those that don't will in most cases get the property at the auction and then you can deal with the REO department of the bank. If there is a second mortgage on the property, you should be able to discount it as much as 98%.

The two key ingredients for a successful short sales are (1) Influencing the BPO so it comes in at a price that is close to your offer price. A BPO is a broker's price opinion which means the lender will hire a real estate broker to give them their opinion on the value of the property. If this number comes in a lot higher than your max offer, the bank will most likely not discount. (2) Providing all necessary documents to the lender including a hardship letter. The short sale package that the lender is requesting must be complete.

If it is incomplete it will be denied. Make sure the homeowner is cooperative so that you can get all the documentation you need. The hardship letter is one of the most important documents. It alone will not convince the lender to accept a short pay off; however, it is one of the key items the lender will review in making a decision. The hardship letter must describe in detail what has caused the homeowner to be in this situation. Provide as many details as possible to make the situation sound bad with no options. Always be sure that the homeowner is truthful in what they write but don't leave out any details.

Follow the instructions from the lender and follow up with the loss mitigation contact until they deny the request or they accept the short payoff. When you are successful at negotiating a discount with

To get the forms discussed in this book and an additional free gift, visit www.fastcashforms.com

the bank, be ready to close quickly. You will either have to have cash lined up to buy the property or you can sell to another cash buyer, but will have to do a double close or simultaneous closing. In this option the seller can receive no proceeds from the sale of the real estate. You can, however, pay them for personal property such as a dishwasher, stove, or refrigerator so that they leave with some cash in their pocket and avoid further damage to their credit.

Summary

As mentioned earlier, you will determine whether or not you want to go see the property based on the equity in the property. It's pretty simple, the property will with fall into two categories enough equity or not enough equity. Here are your options.

Little or No Equity = Don't go pass to realtor (unless you focus on Short Sales)

Enough Equity = Go to Meet with Seller

So, How much equity do you need and how do you determine it? This is what we will discuss in the next Chapter "Deal Analysis".

To get the forms discussed in this book and an additional free gift, visit www.fastcashforms.com

Chapter 6: Equity and Deal Analysis

To determine the equity you figure out how much the property is worth after you fix up the property which is the After Repair Value (ARV) and subtract what you can buy the property for and this will tell you the equity. Later in this chapter we will cover in more detail how to determine the after repaired value.

The amount of equity you will need really depends on what the ARV is for the types of homes you are focused on. The higher the ARV is the more equity you will need. For example if entry levels homes in your area are selling for $100,000 you will need less equity then if they are selling for $200,000. This is because your expenses like taxes, insurance, closing costs when you sell, realtor fee, and financing will be higher for a more expensive home. Let's use the realtor fee as an example. In our area we pay a 5% commission to sell our properties. IF we were selling the property at $100,000 it would cost us $5,000 and if we were selling the property for $200,000, we would have to pay $10,000. As you can see the realtor fee doubled. **Note:** not all of our expense will double but some will.

Let's go through some numbers just to give you an idea of how much equity is enough equity. On the properties that we retail to an end buyer we want to make a minimum profit of 20,000. In my area, if I'm selling houses that have an ARV of $200,000, I know my holding costs are going to be at least $27,000 if I'm buying CASH and assuming I'm holding the property six month. . (I know this because I have analyzed a lot of deals. Later in this chapter we will go over analysis and you will be able to figure out what it is in your area as well.) Therefore, when I'm talking to a seller on the phone and I know his/her property has an ARV of $200,000 I know I need to have at least $47,000 in equity not counting rehab.

To get the forms discussed in this book and an additional free gift, visit www.fastcashforms.com

If the seller tells me they owe $180,000 and the properties ARV is $200,000, then there is only $20,000 in equity and I know I can't buy the property CASH. Just my profit is $20,000 so there is no way it has enough equity. This is just an example to show you how equity works and how you can quickly tell if you have a deal when you get more experienced. The best thing to do or most accurate way to do it is not just to base your decision on equity but to use one of the following analysis techniques so you know exactly what you need to buy the property for before going to the property. This is a big time saver. Determine what you can pay for the property and see what the sellers lowest acceptable price is if it's close to your MAO go see the property.

WHAT'S THE MAXIMUM YOU CAN PAY

There are several methods to determine how much to pay for a property. We use two different methods although the second method is much more accurate and will get you into more deals.

Method 1: 70% Rule

Take the ARV and multiply it by 70% and then subtract the cost of repairs and this equals your maximum allowable offer.

$$\begin{aligned} &\text{After Repaired Value} \\ &\underline{\times\ 70\%} \\ &= \text{subtotal before repairs} \\ &\underline{-\ \text{Repairs}} \\ &= \text{max offer price} \end{aligned}$$

This is a quick formula that is pretty accurate in lower priced homes up to about $150,000. After $150,000 the max offer price may be so low

To get the forms discussed in this book and an additional free gift, visit www.fastcashforms.com

that the seller will not accept the offer. This method will provide you with a healthy profit and cover all the expenses of doing the deal.

Method 2: The offer Calculation/Budget Worksheet

Using this method you will calculate your offer by determining a value for each expense which will allow you to know exactly what your profit will be. In the previous method, you would use 70% to assign a value to the expense of buying, holding, and selling the property. This method breaks down the expenses into several categories to determine a more accurate number. You will also be able to determine your profit as well.

This method will allow you to get into more opportunities and allow you to have a better handle on expenses. At the end of the chapter you will find the offer calculation and budget worksheet. Let's go through the worksheet to determine what each item means and how to use the form.

OFFER CALCULATION WORKSHEET

PROPERTY ADDRESS

Fill in the property address at the top. This may seem simple but as your business increases, you will be working on several opportunities at a time and this will help you ensure you have the right sheets with the right properties.

To get the forms discussed in this book and an additional free gift, visit www.fastcashforms.com

PROPOSED V ACTUAL

There are two columns here, proposed and actual. When you are filling the form out in order to calculate your offer, you will fill all your numbers in the proposed column. After you have bought and sold the property, you will want to fill in the exact numbers for each category. By completing this exercise, you will see any variances between what you expected to happen and what actually happened. Use this information to improve your process and make your offers more accurate.

OFFER CALCULATION WORKSHEET

Property Address:

	Offer Analysis	Actual
Sales Price (ARV)		
Rehab		
Closing Cost - Purchase		
Closing Cost - Sale		
Insurance		
Taxes		
Utilities		
Interest Payments	Rate 0.0% $0	LTV 80%
Broker's Commission 0.0%	$0	
Profit		
Other		
Sub Total Cost	$0	
Purchase Price (MAO)	$0	

Total Profit (Calculate After House has been Sold) _____

Total Daily Carrying Cost
(6 month taxes, insurance, utilities, and interest divided by 180) $0.00   Per Day

To get the forms discussed in this book and an additional free gift, visit www.fastcashforms.com

DETERMINING SALES PRICE (ARV)

This is where you will enter the after repaired value that we covered earlier in this chapter. To determine this value, you will need to find comparable properties that have sold within the past three to six months. You want to pull three types of comps: Active, Pending, and Sold. The active comparables, you will give you an idea of what your current competition is.

The pending comparables are properties that are under agreement and will be closing or selling in the near future. You will not know the price the property is under agreement for and the sales price will not be disclosed until after the closing takes place. Track the pending comps because they will turn into sold comps and you will use them at that time. Finally, the most important will be the sold comparables. The sold comps will tell you what other houses of the same size and features sold for recently.

When searching for comparables, they need to be just that comparable. You must be comparing apples to apples and the more recent they have sold the better.

Some of the categories to consider are:

Location/Neighborhood
Main Road, Side Street, or Cul-de-sac? The most desirable of the three is
the cul-de-sac. The least desirable is the main road. If the subject property is on the main road, you will have to discard the comparables if they are not located on the main road.

To get the forms discussed in this book and an additional free gift, visit www.fastcashforms.com

Commercial Building

Is it near a commercial Building? Location and what is surrounding a property are key to the value of the property and how quickly it will sell.

One Way Street

Houses on a one way street are more difficult to sell because they are slightly harder to get to. It may seem minor to you but may affect the buyer.

Style

You need to make sure that the style is the same. If the subject property is a ranch, then compare it to a ranch. You can't compare it to another house type without adjusting the price. Appraisers do this all the time but they are licensed and trained on how to do it. Play it safe and use the same style for the comps as the subject property.

Beds/Bath

If the subject property has three beds and one bath, then compare it to properties that have the same amount of each.

Square Footage

Be careful when it comes to square footage of the property. The category can be misleading. You want to use comparables with about the same square footage or at least within 200 sq. ft. Just because the house has more square footage than others of the same style or number of beds, it doesn't mean that it is necessarily worth a lot more. The property might have double the square footage of the comps but may have been over improved for the neighborhood. Neighborhoods will max out at a certain price and those that don't fit the neighborhood profile will be worth less per square foot.

To get the forms discussed in this book and an additional free gift, visit www.fastcashforms.com

Days on Market

This is one of the most important items to consider. If you plan to sell the property within 60 days you will want to use comps that sold in about the same number of days. Many investors fall into the trap of using a higher comp to justify the higher after repair value but don't consider the days on market. The days on market are the number of days from the time the property was listed for sale until the day it was sold. Yes, if you wait longer you can get a higher price in some cases, but this is quick turn real estate and we want to sell quickly. Every day that goes by costs you money.

How to Find Sales Comparables

The best source for comparable sales will be the MLS or Multiple Listing Service. In order to access this information you must be a Realtor. If you are not a Realtor, you can still get the information; you just have to ask a Realtor for it. Why would they provide you this information? Realtors are used to working on contingency. Contingency means that they don't get paid unless they sell. In our case, they are willing to pull comps for us because they hope to get the listing when we sell the property. You are in the relationship business, so find a realtor to build a relationship with to get your comps. There are some other sources that are not as reliable as the MLS but they may give you a general idea as to the value such as the tax assessor of the county the property is located in.

In some cases the county will provide other properties that have recently sold that are like the subject property. If they provide sold data, the information is accurate but you will have to see how

To get the forms discussed in this book and an additional free gift, visit www.fastcashforms.com

often they update their database. Another place is www.zillow.com. The information on this website is somewhat accurate. Most of the sold data is correct, however, you need to verify the property specifics as they are sometimes incorrect. The comps that they show may not be in the same neighborhood as the subject property. The information provided can be used to see if you are in the ballpark, however, in order to determine ad ARV when buying, you should only use comparables from the MLS.

DEFINITION OF CATEGORIES

REHAB

This is where you will put the dollar amount of repairs the property needs. In order to determine this, you will need to have a contractor or someone you know with knowledge come to the property with you to determine what it will cost to repair. After you do it a few times you will begin to get better at estimating repairs and what things cost.

CLOSING COSTS PURCHASE

When you purchase a property there will be some costs associated with it. These costs are generally settlement fees, document preparation, title search, and recording fees. A good rule of Thumb to start with is $2500 but the best thing to do is to call a local attorney and find out what is common in your area. This way your analysis will be more accurate..

CLOSING COST SALE

To get the forms discussed in this book and an additional free gift, visit www.fastcashforms.com

When you sell, there will be very few expenses. Most states charge a transfer tax. You will also pay a recording fee and if you choose to have the proceeds wired to you, there will be a wiring fee. A good rule of Thumb to start with is $1500 but the best thing to do is to call a local attorney and find out what is common in your area. This way your analysis will be more accurate.

INSURANCE

The insurance category will be for hazard and liability insurance which is commonly referred to as homeowners insurance. Since the house will be vacant and unoccupied while you own it, you will need a special type of insurance called vacant house insurance. Contact your insurance agent for details about which insurance is right for your situation. You should factor six months of insurance as a rule of thumb. A good rule of Thumb to start with is $1800 for 6 months but the best thing to do is to call an insurance agency and find out what is common in your area. This way your analysis will be more accurate.

TAXES

In this line you will put the amount of property taxes equal to six months. Check to see if there are any other special taxes such as a fire district tax.

UTILITIES

While you own the property you will have to pay the utilities. The common utilities are water, sewer, electric, gas, and oil. A good rule of Thumb to start with is $200/month.

INTEREST PAYMENTS

To get the forms discussed in this book and an additional free gift, visit www.fastcashforms.com

Depending on how you choose to finance the property, you will most likely have an interest payment to make. You might be using hard money, private money, or conventional financing. If you are paying any principal as part of your payment, be sure to deduct it and include only the interest portion of the payment, if you paid any points include these here as well.

BROKER COMMISSION

Even if you plan to sell the property on your own, you want to factor in a real estate sales commission. Find out what is typical in your market and remember it is negotiable. Try to lock in as close to a full commission as possible as this will increase your chances of selling quickly. Many times we will even offer an incentive to the Realtor for getting it under agreement within seven days.

PROFIT

This is where you put the money you will make on a deal. You will have to decide what your minimum profit number is and put that number here. Even if you put a minimum profit number of $20,000 you can always increase it and lower your offer.

OTHER

Anything that did not fall into one of the above categories will go here. I commonly use this category when I am going to wholesale the deal to another investor without closing on the property. I will assign the contract to them and use this category to account for my fee which might be 5k, 7k, 10k, or more. Keep in mind if you are going to

To get the forms discussed in this book and an additional free gift, visit www.fastcashforms.com

assign the contract that the profit in the line above needs to be what your buyer wants for a profit.

SUBTOTAL

Add all the costs up and place them on the subtotal line.

PURCHASE PRICE

Subtract the subtotal cost amount from the sales price to determine your maximum allowable offer(MAO). Now that you have determined your maximum allowable offer, that is the most you want to pay for the property. You might offer something less and then go as high as that number if necessary during negotiations.

TOTAL PROFIT

You will only calculate this after the house is sold and you complete the "actual" column on the worksheet.

TOTAL DAILY CARRYING COSTS

This will give you the yearly carrying cost. Be sure to use six months of the categories listed and then divide by 180 to determine your approximate daily carrying cost. You can use this number to help you make decisions. Post this number on your wall or on your calendar to remind you how much money you are losing each day. This should provide some motivation to get the property sold. Now that we have gone through the offer, calculate, and budget worksheet, you should use it to determine what your maximum offer will be for the properties you will get under contract.

Another useful way to use this form is as a negotiating tool. When you meet with the seller, fill this form out ahead of time so you

To get the forms discussed in this book and an additional free gift, visit www.fastcashforms.com

can finalize the numbers and know what you will use for each category. Instead of just telling them what the offer is, use a blank copy of this form to present the offer. Fill in right in front of them. The goal will be to get agreement every step along the way. So write in a number and explain what it is and how you calculated it and ask them a tie down question such as, "Does that sound like a fair value for the house if it were fixed up?" Get them to say yes and then move on to the next item. By the time you get to the bottom of the worksheet, they will have no choice but to say yes to your offer price.

Some investors are reluctant to show the homeowner all of these numbers because they feel that the seller will see how much money the investor is making. It is okay for them to know. What we like about this worksheet is that it shows them what our real profit is. For example, when you tell someone that your offer is $150,000 and the neighbor just sold their house for $210,000 they think that you are making $60,000. In that example, you will have about $30,000 in expenses $10,000 in rehab, and only $20,000 in profit.

By using this technique of showing them all the numbers you just showed them, you are not making $60,000, you are really making $20,000, which is a third of what it might have looked like if you had not explained the offer in detail. Most sellers will understand that you are in business to make a profit and this is how you support your family.

To get the forms discussed in this book and an additional free gift, visit www.fastcashforms.com

Chapter 7: Preparing for your Visit

Now that you have determined over the phone that the seller is motivated and willing to accept an offer close to or below your MAO, you need to be prepared to go to the appointment. Our primary buying method in the quick turn business is "CASH" because as mentioned earlier "CASH" is king. . In this chapter we cover all the documentation that you need to bring with you and what you need to have the seller sign when you are doing a "CASH" transaction.

DOCUMENTATON YOU WILL NEED WHEN BUYING CASH

Authorization to release information : (You only need to use this doc if the seller is behind on payments or if the price they are willing to accept is close to what the seller owes) Even when you are buying all cash you still need to get this document. This document will allow you to communicate with the seller's lender and also obtain a loan payoff amount. Before I invest too much time in the deal, I want to make sure that their payoff amount is close to what they thought it was. In some cases the payoff will be higher than the price you negotiated leaving them with nothing. In that case you will need to go back and renegotiate or start a short sale.

If the seller will be getting less money than they thought at the closing, you will want to address that as soon as you get the payoff so that you won't have an issue at the closing table. When buying for

To get the forms discussed in this book and an additional free gift, visit www.fastcashforms.com

cash, this document will be instrumental to having a smooth closing where everyone leaves happy.

Purchase and Sales Agreement:

This will be the document that you and the seller sign agreeing in writing to sell the property under certain terms laid out in the document. If you plan on recording the P & S at the courthouse to prevent the seller from selling to someone else, you may need to have the P & S notarized. If you are going to record at the courthouse, it would be wise to record a memorandum of agreement rather than disclose to the world the terms of your agreement.

An example of a purchase and sales agreement is included in the next few pages however you should consult an attorney in the state you are doing business in to make sure the document meets the laws of the state.

Seller Property Disclosure

Your state may call it something different but this is the form that the seller fills out to disclose any problems with the house and any previous damage such as fire or flood or pest infestation. Even though you are buying as is, and they may not completely fill out the form, it may jog their memory about certain things they left out especially things like underground oil tanks. This is one of the most important items.

Seller Acknowledgement

To get the forms discussed in this book and an additional free gift, visit www.fastcashforms.com

This form is used just to show that you are conducting business with integrity and you are not trying to take advantage of people in motivated situations. They are basically confirming on this form that they are not being forced into an agreement, they are not confused by anything, you are in business to make a profit, and it's in their best interest to sell the property given their situation.

Property Inspection Sheet

This is the form you filled out at the property as you toured each room and the exterior of the house. This form will be helpful to refer to; and after you visit two to three houses per day, they will all blend together. Use the information on this sheet to provide a scope of work to contractors for repairs to be done you can also use it to tell your private lenders what type of repairs it needs or tell other investors that you are wholesaling the property to. (Example in next chapter)

Offer Calculation Worksheet

This form was covered in detail earlier in the last chapter. This form will be an instrumental part in convincing the homeowner to sell for the price you are offering. The form will also be used to conduct an analysis of your budgeted numbers to determine actual profit.

Process when Buying "ALL CASH"

You will meet with the seller on two different occasions. At the first meeting you sign the initial documents described on the previous pages.

    Authorization to Release Information
    Purchase and Sales agreement
    Seller Property Disclosure

To get the forms discussed in this book and an additional free gift, visit www.fastcashforms.com

The second meeting will occur after the seller has moved out and the property is in broom swept condition. This meeting will usually take place at your attorney's office or your title company's office. The closing will be described in a later chapter.

AUTHORIZATION TO RELEASE

Date _____

To: (Lender) _____

RE: (Mortgagors Name(s):
_____

Property Address _____
                 _____

Account Number: _____

Lending Institution Phone Number:
_____

TO WHOM IT MAY CONCERN:

The undersigned hereby authorizes you to provide mortgage reinstatement figures, mortgage payoff figures and information to:

Craig Picard
123 Main St.
Providence RI, 02909
Office: 401-555-5786
Fax: 877-555-9999

_____   _____
Signature   Signature

_____   _____
Print   Print

_____   _____
Social Security #   Social Security #

To get the forms discussed in this book and an additional free gift, visit www.fastcashforms.com

STANDARD REAL ESTATE PURCHASE AND SALE AGREEMENT

Parties

_____, hereinafter referred to as Buyer, and _____, hereinafter referred to as Seller, which terms may be singular or plural and include the heirs, successors, personal representatives and assigns of Seller and Buyer, hereby agree that Seller will sell and Buyer will buy the following property, with such improvements as are located thereon, and is described as follows: Address: _____ City: _____ State: _____ Zip: _____

Seller will sell and Buyer will buy upon the following terms and conditions, if completed or marked. On any conflict of terms or conditions, that which is added will supersede that which is printed or marked. It is understood that the Property will be conveyed by General Warranty Deed (unless otherwise specified in paragraph 17), with covenants, restrictions, and easements of record.

1. **Total Purchase Price** to be paid by Buyer is payable as follows:

    A. Earnest money deposit check [ ] or promissory note [ ], which will
    remain as a binder until closing, and be held for Seller by closing agent
    (chosen by Buyer) for Seller until closing, unless sooner forfeited or
    returned, according to the provisions of this Agreement.

    B. Balance due at closing (not including Buyers closing costs, prepaid items
    or prorations) in U.S. cash or locally drawn certified or cashiers check.
                              approximately [ ]: exactly [ ]

    C. Proceeds of a new loan to be executed by Buyer to any lender other than
    Seller; Name of Lender: _____

    D. Seller financing as herein set forth in paragraph 14.
                              approximately [ ]: exactly [ ]

To get the forms discussed in this book and an additional free gift, visit www.fastcashforms.com

E. "Subject to" existing loan balance encumbering the Property
Lender _____ Loan # _____
Interest Rate _____ % Fixed Rate [ ] Adjustable Rate [ ] $ _____ /month
Includes Principal [ ]; Interest [ ]; Escrow: Taxes [ ]; Insurance [ ]

F. "Subject to" existing second loan balance encumbering the Property $ _____
Lender _____ Loan # _____
Interest Rate _____ % Fixed Rate [ ] Adjustable Rate [ ] P&I $ _____ per month

G. Total Purchase Price.   approximately [ ] exactly [ ]

2. Seller Will Pay: Seller will pay all closing costs to include: Recording Fees, Intangibles Tax, Credit Reports, Funding Fee, Loan Origination Fee, Document Preparation Fee, Loan Insurance Premium, Loan Discount, Title Insurance Policy, Attorney's Fees, Courier Fees, Overnight Fee, Appraisal Fee, Survey, Transfer Tax, Satisfaction and Recording Fees, Wood Destroying Organism Report and any other costs associated with the funding or closing of this Agreement, Buyer will pay all additional monies. All taxes, rentals, condominium or association fees, monthly mortgage insurance premiums and interest on loans will be prorated as of the date of closing.

3. Payment of Expenses: If Buyer fails to perform, all loan and sale processing and closing costs incurred, whether the same were to be paid by Seller or Buyer will be the responsibility of the Buyer, with costs deducted from binder deposit. If Seller fails to perform, all loan, fee obligations, appraisal, survey, credit report, application, sales processing and closing costs incurred whether the same were to be paid by Seller or Buyer will be the responsibility of Seller; and Buyer will be entitled to the return of the binder deposit. This will include, but not be limited to the transaction not being closed because Seller is unwilling to complete the transaction, or because Seller elects not to pay for the excess amount in paragraph 8 (with respect to repairs) or because Seller cannot deliver marketable title.

4. Prorations: Any accrued loan interest shall be prorated to the date of closing. Seller will assign to Buyer, at no cost to Buyer, Seller's escrow account and property hazard insurance policy, and/or any refunds which may issue, in lieu of proration of all taxes, association fees, monthly hazard insurance premiums, and monthly mortgage insurance premiums as of the date of closing. Seller will bring any escrow shortage current at closing. In the absence of an escrow account, taxes shall be prorated as the date of closing. If this is rental property, rents are to be prorated as of the date of closing and any deposits of any kind or nature are to be transferred to Buyer at closing.

5. Wood Destroying Organism Report: "Wood Destroying Organism" means any arthropod or plant life, which damages a structure. Seller will have property inspected by a State Certified Pest Control Firm, within seven (7) days of this Agreement, to determine whether there is any visible active wood destroying organism infestation or visible existing structural damage from wood destroying organisms to the improvements. Buyer will be informed of either or both of the foregoing and Seller will have seven (7) days from receipt of written notice thereof within which to have all such wood destroying organism damages whether visible or not inspected and estimated by a licensed

To get the forms discussed in this book and an additional free gift, visit www.fastcashforms.com

building or general contractor. Seller will pay costs of treatment and repair of all structural damage up to one percent (1%) of the purchase price. If such costs exceed the amount agreed to be paid by Seller and Seller declines to treat and repair, Buyer will have the option of (a) terminating this Agreement, (b) proceeding with the transaction, in which event Seller will bear costs equal to one percent (1%) of the purchase price.

6. Title Examination, Place and Time for Closing: A. If title evidence and survey show Seller is vested with a good, clear and marketable title, subject to permitted title exceptions contained in a national title insurance company commitment at its standard rates (permitted exceptions are for restrictive covenants, leases, survey, current taxes, zoning ordinances and easements of record), the transaction will be closed and the deed and other closing papers delivered on or before _____, 20___, plus any extensions necessary in order to complete paperwork, unless extended by other conditions of this Agreement or this Agreement is canceled by the Buyer. Buyer shall select closing attorney or title company. B. If title evidence or survey reveal any defects which render the title unclear, Buyer will have 7 days from receipt of title commitment and survey to notify Seller of such title defects and Seller agrees to use reasonable diligence (including payment of money) to cure such defects at Seller's expense and will have 30 days to do so, in which event this transaction will be closed within 10 days after delivery to Buyer of evidence that such defects have been cured. Seller agrees to pay for and discharge all due or delinquent taxes, liens and other encumbrances, unless otherwise agreed. If Seller is unable to convey to Buyer a good, clear and marketable title, Buyer will have the right to terminate this Agreement, at the same time returning to Seller all title evidence and surveys received from Seller, OR Buyer shall have the right to renegotiate this agreement with Seller and accept such title as Seller may be able to convey, which election will be exercised within 10 days from notice of Seller's inability to cure. Closing attorney or title company will then close upon the modified agreement. Seller agrees to execute a "Notice of Purchase and Sale Agreement" so that the Buyer may protect their interest in the contract herein.

7. Loss or Damage: If the property is damaged by fire or other casualty prior to closing, and cost of restoration does not exceed 3% of the assessed valuation of the improvements located on the Property, cost of restoration will be an obligation of the Seller and closing will proceed pursuant to the terms of this Agreement with cost thereof escrowing at closing. In the event cost of restoration exceeds 3% of the assessed valuation of the improvements and Seller declines to repair or restore, Buyer will have the option of either taking the Property as is, together with either the said 3% or any insurance proceeds payable by virtue of such loss or damage, with Seller paying Buyer in cash any insurance deductible, OR of canceling this Agreement.

8. Property Condition and Inspection: Seller shall deliver the Property in the same condition as they were on the date of this Agreement, normal wear and tear excepted, and they shall be in a clean and ready to occupy condition, except as otherwise specified herein. Seller further certifies and represents that Seller knows of no latent defects to the Property and knows of no facts materially affecting the value of the Property except the following:

_____
___

_____

This Agreement is subject to an inspection of the Property and approval by Buyer and/or his associates after acceptance of this Agreement by Seller. If not already on, Seller shall have all

To get the forms discussed in this book and an additional free gift, visit www.fastcashforms.com

utilities on for inspection and shall notify Buyer when they are on. In the event any system, appliance, roof, foundation or structural member, etc., shall be found defective, Buyer shall notify Seller at or prior to closing and Seller shall thereupon remedy the defect forthwith at his sole expense (in which case the time for closing shall be extended as may reasonably be necessary) or, in the event the cost of such repairs shall exceed 5% of the "Total Purchase Price", Seller may elect not to make such repairs and Buyer may elect to renegotiate this Agreement, accepting such amount as Seller may agree to pay, then take the Property in its "AS-IS' condition, OR terminate this Agreement and receive a full refund of all earnest monies hereunder. Seller guarantees that the appliances remaining with the dwelling and the heating, air conditioning, plumbing and electrical systems, where applicable, will be in operating condition at the time of closing.

9. Occupancy: Seller represents that there are no parties in occupancy other than Seller and Buyer will be given occupancy at closing. Any belongings, furniture or fixtures on property after closing shall be considered as abandoned and Buyer shall have the right of disposal of same. Any tenant, if appropriate, shall be terminated and shall have vacated the Property prior to the closing of this Agreement, unless otherwise agreed to by Buyer in writing.

10. Personal Property: Included in the purchase price are all fixed equipment including all window treatments, built-in appliances, refrigerator, floor coverings, stove, air conditioner(s), ceiling fans, attached lighting fixtures, mailbox, fence, storage building, plants, yard
ornaments and shrubbery as now installed on the property, and these additional items which will be conveyed by Bill of Sale at the closing:
_____
_____

Items specifically excluded from this Agreement:
_____
_____

11. Default and Attorney's Fees: If Buyer defaults on this Agreement, all deposits will be retained by the Seller as full settlement of any claim, whereupon Buyer and Seller will be relieved of all obligations under this Agreement. If Seller defaults under this Agreement, the Buyer may seek specific performance or elect to receive the return of the Buyer's binder deposit(s) without thereby waiving any action for damages resulting from Seller's breach. If Seller refuses to sell for any reason other than those outlined herein, Seller and Buyer herewith agree that this Agreement, and all transaction contemplated hereby, shall be governed by, construed and enforced in accordance with applicable state law. Any and all claims, controversies or disputes arising out of or relating to this Agreement, or the breach thereof, which remain unresolved after direct negotiations between the Parties, shall first be submitted to confidential mediation in accordance with the rules, procedures, and protocols for mediation of disputes under applicable state law then in effect upon ten (10) days notice via both certified and regular mail, one party unto the other. If any issues, claims or disputes remain unresolved after mediation concludes, the Parties hereto agree to immediately submit any such issues to binding

To get the forms discussed in this book and an additional free gift, visit www.fastcashforms.com

arbitration before one/three arbitrator(s) in accordance with the rules, procedures, and protocols for arbitration of disputes under applicable state law then in effect. The parties further agree that the award of the arbitrator(s) is binding upon the Parties and that all expenses of such mediation and/or arbitration shall be borne by the losing Party and that any judgment upon the award rendered may be entered, after ten (10) days, into any court of competent jurisdiction.

12. Zoning and Restrictions: Seller warrants Property is zoned residential. Should Buyer discover any proposed zoning change unacceptable to Buyer, Buyer may void this Agreement.

13. Maintenance and Access: Until title is delivered, Seller agrees to maintain all heating, sewer, plumbing and electrical systems and any appliances remaining with the Property, and other equipment in normal working order and to keep the roof water tight and to maintain the grounds. Buyer has the right to make repairs, show the Property to prospects, lenders, contractors or partners, and to post signs for sale, rental or rent to own before closing.

14. Purchase Money Note: Seller agrees to take back a Purchase Money Note, as contained in paragraph 1D, for the amount of $_____ for a period of _____ months. Payments, which include principal and interest, are $_____ due _____ and shall start/be payable on _____, 20____. In the event of default, Seller must notify Buyer, in writing by certified mail, of default, and give Buyer 30 days to cure default. This property shall stand as sole security for the Purchase Money Note. Buyer may at any time, without penalty, pay in part or in full the principal balance of the Purchase Money Note owing to Seller. Buyer has the right to substitute like collateral of equal or greater value. Should Seller decide to sell Purchase Money Note, the Buyer shall have the first right of refusal to buy Seller's interest. Any mortgage created by this transaction must include agreed provisions above and be acceptable to Buyer.

15. Survival of Agreement: This Agreement shall survive the closing, execution and delivery of the Warranty Deed, as agreed herein by the undersigned. Buyer intends to buy, sell, rent or trade for a profit.

Assignment: Parties hereto agree that Buyer shall have the right to assign this Agreement and the terms and provisions hereof shall be binding upon and inure to the benefit of the parties hereto, their successors, representatives, heirs and assigns.

17. Buyer's Right to Show. Seller gives Buyer permission to enter property after the date of acceptance for the purpose of showing it to contractors, inspectors, and potential occupants. Seller agrees to make the property available for showing with in 24 hours of a verbal or written request.

18. Additional Terms, Conditions or Exhibits (lettered A, B, C, D, etc.)

IF FINAL BALANCE SHOWN BY LENDER'S STATEMENT OF ACCOUNT SHOWS A LOWER PRINCIPAL BALANCE, THEN THE PURCHASE PRICE SHALL BE REDUCED BY THIS AMOUNT. IF THE STATEMENT SHOWS A HIGHER BALANCE, THEN THE CASH DUE FROM BUYER AT CLOSING SHALL BE REDUCED. IF NO CASH IS DUE, THEN THE SELLER AGREES TO PAY ANY SHORTAGE AT CLOSING.

To get the forms discussed in this book and an additional free gift, visit www.fastcashforms.com

19. There are no other agreements, promises or understandings between these parties except as specifically set forth herein. This legal and binding Agreement will be construed under _____ Law and if not understood, parties should seek competent legal advice. If any signature is faxed or digitally produced it shall have the same legal force and effect as an original ink signature. **TIME IS OF ESSENCE IN THIS AGREEMENT.**

Signed, sealed on the date herein stated. **Show Seller's name (s) as it appear (s) on existing deed, if available.**

Buyer _____   Date _____

Buyer _____   Date _____

Seller_____   Date _____

Seller_____   Date _____

To get the forms discussed in this book and an additional free gift, visit www.fastcashforms.com

REAL ESTATE DISCLOSURE FORM

SELLER INFO

DATE _____ PROPERTY ADDRESS _____
Seller _____ Current Address _____

Seller has occupied **subject** property? Yes _____ No _____ If yes, number of years and when: _____

"Prior to the signing of an agreement to transfer real estate (vacant land or real property and improvements consisting of a house or building containing one (1) to four (4) dwelling units, Seller is providing Buyer with this written disclosure of all deficient conditions of which Seller has knowledge. This is not a warranty by Seller that no other defective conditions exist, which there may or may not be. Buyer should estimate the cost of repair or replacement of deficient conditions prior to submitting an offer on this real estate. Buyer is advised however not to rely solely upon the representation of Seller made in this disclosure, but to conduct any inspections or investigations which Buyer deems to be necessary to protect his or her best interest." Nothing contained herein shall be construed to impose an affirmative duty on the Seller to conduct inspections as to the condition of this real estate.

STRUCTURE

Place a check mark for "Yes" or "No," or mark "UK" (Unknown), if you do not have actual knowledge of the property conditions.

1. **Year Built** _____ Addition(s):_____ Year(s):_____
2. **Roof (Shingles)** Age: _____ # of Layers:_____ Previous Repairs: _____ Known Defects:_____
3. **Fireplaces** # _____ # Working:_____ Maintenance History:_____
4. **Wood/Coal/Gas Stove(s)** Yes ___ No ___ If yes, Type _____ When installed? _____ Permit received? Yes ____ No ____
   If yes, attach copy_____
5. **Insulation** Wall/Type:_____ Ceiling/Type:_____ Floor/Type:_____ Unknown _____
   Ureaformaldehyde Insulation: Yes _____ No _____ Unknown _____
6. **Electrical Service** Fuses _____ Circuit Breakers _____ Amps _____ Unknown _____
   Type: Aluminum Wiring _____ Knob & Tube _____ BX Cable _____ Romex _____ Other _____ Unknown _____
7. **Heating System** Type:_____ Age:_____ If oil fuel, size of tank: _____ Number of zones: _____
   Underground tanks on property? Yes _____ (Size?)_____ No _____ Unknown _____
   Supplemental heating? Yes _____ No _____ If yes, type? _____
8. **Domestic Hot Water** Heating Source: _____ If a separate tank, capacity:_____ gal. Age _____
   Rented? Yes _____ No _____ If yes, Company rented from _____
9. **Air Conditioning** Central Air _____ Number of zones _____ Window Units _____ Number of units ____ Age _____
   Location _____ Maintenance History _____

Additional Structural Information (Attach additional sheets if necessary.)
_____
_____

UTILITIES

10. **Sewage System** Type (private, public or both):_____ If public system available, is it connected? Yes _____ No _____
    If public, Outstanding Assess.? Yes _____ No _____ Minimum Annual Fee: $ _____ Balance $_____
    If private, Cesspool _____ Septic _____ Leach field _____ Galleys _____ Unknown _____ Other _____
    #Bedrooms/per ISDS Design:_____ Copy Available? Yes _____ No _____
    Location:_____ Date installed:_____
    Maintenance History (Any Failure):_____ Sanitation Company used:_____
    Last pumped: _____ Other Connections (Drywell, etc.):_____
11. **Water System** Public _____ Filtration System? Yes _____ No _____
    Private _____ If private: "Buyer understands that this property is, or will be served by a private water supply (well) which may be susceptible to contamination, availability, and potentially harmful to health. If a public water supply is not available, the private water supply must be tested
    Dug well or drilled well? _____ Depth:_____ Location:_____
    Well water inspection certificate available? Yes _____ No _____ If yes, attach copy
    Water Quality Problems? Yes (Explain) _____ No _____
    Filtration System? Yes _____ No _____ Treatment System? Yes_____ No _____

Additional Utilities Information (Attach additional sheets if necessary.)
_____
_____

SELLER'S INITIALS_____ BUYER'S INITIALS_____

To get the forms discussed in this book and an additional free gift, visit
www.fastcashforms.com

MUNICIPAL INFORMATION

12. **Property Tax $** _____ for fiscal/calendar year ending _____ Tax Rate: _____ Current Exemptions: _____
13. **Easements** Seller is legally required to provide the Buyer with a copy of any previous surveys of the property that are in the Seller's possession and notify the Buyer of any known easements, encroachments, covenants or restrictions of the Seller's property. A Buyer may wish to have a boundary or other survey independently performed at Buyer's expense.
Does Seller have a copy of any surveys in his/her possession? Yes _____ No _____ If yes, attach copy
Does Seller have any knowledge of Easement(s) or Right(s) of Way on property? Yes _____ No _____
If yes, describe _____
Does Seller have any knowledge of Encroachments? Yes _____ No _____
If yes, describe _____
14. **Deed** Type of deed to be conveyed: _____ Number of parcels conveying: _____
15. **Zoning** "Buyers are legally obligated to comply with all local real estate ordinances; including, but not limited to ordinances on the number of unrelated persons who may legally reside in a dwelling, as well as ordinances on the number of dwelling units permitted under the local zoning ordinances. If the subject property is located in a historic district, that fact must be disclosed to the buyer, together with the notification that property located in a historic district may be subject to construction, expansion, or renovation limitations. Contact the local building inspection official for details."
Classification: _____ Is the current use a permitted use under the current zoning regulations? Yes ___ No ___ Unknown ___ If no, explain: _____
Is the current use non-conforming in any other way? Yes _____ No _____ Unknown _____
If yes, explain: _____
16. **Restrictions** Plat or other? Yes (Explain) _____ No _____ Copy available to Buyer: _____
17. **Building Permits** Have you applied for or been granted a special permit for this property? Yes _____ No _____
If yes, explain: _____
Have building permits been obtained for all required construction and/or renovation while you have owned the property? Yes _____ No _____ If no, explain: _____
18. **Building Code/or Minimum Housing** Violations: _____
19. **Flood Plain** Is the property located in a flood plain? Yes _____ No _____ Unknown _____
Is there flood insurance on the property? Yes _____ No _____ If yes, $ _____ per year.
20. **Wetlands** The location of coastal wetlands, bays, fresh water wetlands, ponds, marshes, or swamps, and the associated buffer areas may impact future property development. If known, Seller must disclose to the Buyer any such determination on all or part of the land made by the Department of Environmental Management.
Has all or part of property been determined to be coastal wetland, bog, freshwater wetland, pond, marsh, river bank or swamp? Yes
(Explain) _____
No _____ Unknown _____

Additional Municipal Information (Attach additional sheets if necessary.) _____
_____
_____

CONDO / MULTI UNIT

22. **Condo/Assoc. Fees** Monthly Condo/Association Fee: $ _____ Heat/Electric/Water Included in Fee? _____
Working Capital Deposit? Yes _____ No _____ If yes, Amount: $ _____ Buyer to pay? Yes _____ No _____
Current Outstanding Assessments: $ _____
Fire Alarm System up to date? Yes _____ No _____ Unknown _____
Anticipated Future Assessments: Yes _____ If yes, describe _____ No _____ Unknown _____
23. **Multi-family or Other RentalProperty** Are income and expense figures available? Yes _____ No _____ If yes, attach copies
Lease(s) period: _____ Copies available? Yes _____ No _____ Number of Units: _____
Are the existing rents current? Yes _____ No _____ Security Deposits _____
Are all units legal for the current zoning and use? Yes _____ No _____
Appliances Offered: _____

Additional Condo/Multi Unit Information (Attach additional sheets if necessary.) _____
_____
_____
_____

SELLER'S INITIALS _____ BUYER'S INITIALS _____

To get the forms discussed in this book and an additional free gift, visit
www.fastcashforms.com

NOTICES /DISCLOSURES

24. **Pools & Equipment**   Age of pool:_____ Maintenance history:_____
    Was a permit obtained for the pool? Yes _____ No _____ Unknown _____

25. **Lead Contamination**   "Every Purchaser of any interest in residential property is notified that such property may present exposure to lead from lead-based hazards that may place young children at risk of developing lead poisoning. Lead poisoning in young children may produce permanent neurological damage, including learning disabilities, reduced Intelligence Quotient, behavioral problems, and impaired memory. Lead poisoning also poses a particular risk to pregnant women. The Seller of any interest in residential property is required to provide the Buyer with any information on lead or lead hazards in paint, interior dust, soil, or water from risk assessments or inspections in the Seller's possession and notify the Buyer of any known or potential lead or lead-based hazards, and must receive a lead disclosure and educational brochure. A risk assessment or inspection for possible lead-based hazards is recommended prior to purchase." Have you ever had a lead paint inspection conducted? Yes _____ No _____
    If yes, copy of report available? Yes _____ No _____
    Lead compliance certificate(s) available? Yes _____ No _____

26. **Smoke/ Carbon Monoxide**   Installed and functioning? Yes _____ No _____ Seller of a 1 to 3 unit property is required to provide certificate from the local fire official prior to closing.

27. **Radon**   "Radon has been determined to exist in the State of Rhode Island. Testing for the presence of Radon in residential real estate prior to purchase is advisable."
    Has building been tested for Radon? Yes _____ No _____ If yes, # of Pico curies/liter: _____
    Copy of test available? Yes _____ No _____ Any action taken? _____

Additional Notices/Disclosures Information (Attach additional sheets if necessary.) _____
_____
_____

STRUCTURE

Do any defects/malfunctions exist in any of the following? Mark Yes (Y), No (N), Unknown (UK) or Not Applicable (NA).

#	Y N UK NA	Item	#	Y N UK NA	Item	#	Y N UK NA	Item
28	☐ ☐ ☐ ☐	Basement	34	☐ ☐ ☐ ☐	Driveway(s)	39	☐ ☐ ☐ ☐	Plumbing
29	☐ ☐ ☐ ☐	Bulkhead/Hatchway	35	☐ ☐ ☐ ☐	Exterior Walls	40	☐ ☐ ☐ ☐	Sidewalks
30	☐ ☐ ☐ ☐	Ceilings	36	☐ ☐ ☐ ☐	Floors	41	☐ ☐ ☐ ☐	Walls/Fences
31	☐ ☐ ☐ ☐	Chimney(s)	37	☐ ☐ ☐ ☐	Foundation/Slab(s)	42	☐ ☐ ☐ ☐	Windows
32	☐ ☐ ☐ ☐	Doors	38	☐ ☐ ☐ ☐	Interior Walls			
33	☐ ☐ ☐ ☐	Other Structural Components (Describe) _____						

If the answer to any of the items is Yes (Y), please explain. (Attach additional sheets if necessary.) _____
_____
_____

EQUIPMENT

Does any item, equipment or system in or on the property and <u>conveying with the sale</u> need repair or replacement? Mark Yes (Y), No (N), Unknown (UK) or Not Applicable (NA).

#	Y N UK NA	Item	#	Y N UK NA	Item	#	Y N UK NA	Item
43	☐ ☐ ☐ ☐	Alarm/Security System	51	☐ ☐ ☐ ☐	Generator	59	☐ ☐ ☐ ☐	Satellite Dish
44	☐ ☐ ☐ ☐	Ceiling/Whole House Fan	52	☐ ☐ ☐ ☐	Hot Tub/Sauna	60	☐ ☐ ☐ ☐	Sump Pump
45	☐ ☐ ☐ ☐	Central Vac/Equipment	53	☐ ☐ ☐ ☐	Intercom System	61	☐ ☐ ☐ ☐	Trash Compactor
46	☐ ☐ ☐ ☐	Dishwasher	54	☐ ☐ ☐ ☐	Jacuzzi/Whirlpool	62	☐ ☐ ☐ ☐	Washer
47	☐ ☐ ☐ ☐	Dryer	55	☐ ☐ ☐ ☐	Kitchen Stove/Oven	63	☐ ☐ ☐ ☐	_____
48	☐ ☐ ☐ ☐	Freezer	56	☐ ☐ ☐ ☐	Lawn Sprinkler System	64	☐ ☐ ☐ ☐	_____
49	☐ ☐ ☐ ☐	Garage Door Opener(s)	57	☐ ☐ ☐ ☐	Lighting Fixtures	65	☐ ☐ ☐ ☐	_____
50	☐ ☐ ☐ ☐	Garbage Disposal	58	☐ ☐ ☐ ☐	Refrigerator	66	☐ ☐ ☐ ☐	_____

If the answer to any of the items is Yes (Y), please explain. (Attach additional sheets if necessary.) _____
_____
_____

SELLER'S INITIALS _____ **BUYER'S INITIALS** _____

To get the forms discussed in this book and an additional free gift, visit
www.fastcashforms.com

CONDITION

Do any of the following conditions exist? Yes (Y), No (N), Unknown (UK) or Not Applicable (NA).

	Y	N	UK	NA			Y	N	UK	NA	
67	☐	☐	☐	☐	Asbestos	81	☐	☐	☐	☐	Water Penetration
68	☐	☐	☐	☐	Cemetery or Burial Ground on Property	82	☐	☐	☐	☐	Wood Rot
69	☐	☐	☐	☐	Diseased Tree(s) within 100' of Dwelling/Outbuilding						Previous Flooding:
70	☐	☐	☐	☐	Endangered Species/Habitat on Property	83	☐	☐	☐	☐	Into the Improvements
71	☐	☐	☐	☐	Hazardous or Toxic Waste	84	☐	☐	☐	☐	Onto the Property
72	☐	☐	☐	☐	Hazardous or Toxic Waste Site Within 1 Mile						Structural Repairs:
73	☐	☐	☐	☐	Improper Drainage	85	☐	☐	☐	☐	Previous Foundation Repairs
74	☐	☐	☐	☐	Landfill	86	☐	☐	☐	☐	Other Structural Repairs
75	☐	☐	☐	☐	Mold						Termites or Other Wood-Destroying Insects:
76	☐	☐	☐	☐	Previous Fire/Smoke Damage	87	☐	☐	☐	☐	Active Infestation
77	☐	☐	☐	☐	Settling	88	☐	☐	☐	☐	Previous Treatment
78	☐	☐	☐	☐	Soil Movement	89	☐	☐	☐	☐	Previous Damage Repaired
79	☐	☐	☐	☐	Subsurface Structure(s) or Pit(s)	90	☐	☐	☐	☐	Damage Needing Repair
80	☐	☐	☐	☐	Synthetic Stucco / EIFS	91	☐	☐	☐	☐	Current Service Contract

If the answer to any of the conditions is Yes (Y), please explain. (Attach additional sheets if necessary.) _____
_____
_____

COMMENTS

Additional Comments: _____
_____
_____

Changes since property was first listed: _____
_____
_____

Date _____ Seller's Initials _____   Date _____ Buyer's Initials _____

STATEMENT

Any agreement to transfer real estate shall contain an acknowledgment that a completed real estate disclosure form has been provided to the Buyer by the Seller in accordance with the provisions of this section. Seller acknowledges that the above property information is accurate, true and complete to the best of his knowledge, and that no information concerning the property has been knowingly withheld. Seller further acknowledges that the legal and/or tax consequences of this real estate sale and all transactions related thereto may be best discussed with an attorney, accountant, or other appropriate party and that Seller has not relied on the Buyer for such advice. **Seller is obligated to report to the Buyer any known changes prior to sales agreement and prior to closing.**

ACKNOWLEDGEMENT

Seller hereby acknowledges that the information set forth above is true and accurate to the best of my (our) knowledge. Buyer/Prospective Buyer acknowledges receipt of Seller's Disclosure Form before purchase.

Date _____ Seller _____   Date _____ Seller _____

Date _____ Buyer _____   Date _____ Buyer _____

SELLER'S INITIALS _____ BUYER'S INITIALS _____

To get the forms discussed in this book and an additional free gift, visit www.fastcashforms.com

SELLER ACKNOWLEDGEMENTS

I _____ (Seller), on this _____ day of _____, 2008, have agreed in writing to sell the property commonly known as _____,(The Property) to _____ and or assigns (Buyer), according to the terms and conditions contained in the Purchase and Sale Agreement (The Agreement) of even date, a copy of which is attached hereto. I further state as follows:

_____ **1. OWNERSHIP OF THE PROPERTY:** I am the owner of The Property (or I

have an equitable interest in The Property) and am able to contract for its sale.

_____ **2. ACCEPTANCE:** I have reviewed the terms and conditions contained in

The Agreement and have accepted Buyer's offer to purchase The Property.

_____ **3. GOOD AND VALUABLE CONSIDERATION:** I have received good and

valuable consideration in signing The Agreement, and I acknowledge both the receipt and the sufficiency of the consideration.

_____ **4. IN MY BEST INTEREST:** I am satisfied with The Agreement and have

agreed to sell The Property because it is in my best interest to do so.

_____ **5. FULLY INFORMED AND NOT CONFUSED:** I have signed The

Agreement being fully informed and with sufficient understanding of all terms and conditions

To get the forms discussed in this book and an additional free gift, visit www.fastcashforms.com

contained therein. I am not confused about any aspect of The Agreement.

_____ **6. SATISFIED WITH THE SALES PRICE:** I understand I may be selling

The Property for less than market value but have chosen to do so because circumstances

dictate that an immediate sale, even at a discounted price, is in my best interest. I am

satisfied with the sales price I have negotiated.

_____ **7. SALE IS FINAL:** I understand by signing The Agreement, I have agreed

to sell The Property to Buyer and am now bound by the terms and conditions described in

The Agreement. I further understand that I cannot "change my mind" or cancel the contract

at some later date, nor can I continue to market The Property to any other buyer.

_____ **8. CONTINGENCIES MAY EXIST:** I understand the sale may be contingent

upon Buyer's inspection and approval of certain items described in The Agreement. I further

understand that if Buyer does not approve of these items, Buyer may cancel The Agreement

and if cancelled, I must return Buyer's earnest money in full.

_____ **9. NOT A LOAN:** I understand The Agreement I have signed is for the

To get the forms discussed in this book and an additional free gift, visit www.fastcashforms.com

outright sale of The Property and is not intended to be a loan of any kind.

_____ **10. AGREEMENT MAY BE ASSIGNED:** I understand Buyer may assign The

Agreement to another party and I may be closing the sale with someone other than Buyer.

_____ **11. NO ESCROW:** I understand Buyer may choose to "close" this transaction

without the use of an escrow company and may record the conveyance documents himself.

_____ **12. CLOSING DOCUMENTS:** I understand there will be additional closing

documents to sign and upon receipt, agree to sign and deliver the closing documents either

into Escrow or directly to Buyer, as Buyer may direct, in a timely manner.

_____ **13. COPIES OF THE PAPERWORK:** I understand that copies of the

paperwork I've signed will be provided to me in a timely manner and I acknowledge that

circumstances dictate that copies may not be immediately made available to me.

_____ **14. BUYER ENTITLED TO MAKE A PROFIT:** I understand Buyer may resell

The Property and may realize a profit in doing so. I agree Buyer is entitled to any profit that

may ultimately result in the subsequent resale of The Property.

To get the forms discussed in this book and an additional free gift, visit www.fastcashforms.com

_____ **15. LEGAL COUNSEL ADVISED:** I acknowledge Buyer has advised me to

seek independent legal counsel to review The Agreement.

_____ **16. FAIRLY NEGOTIATED:** I understand Buyer has negotiated on his own

behalf and likewise, I have negotiated on mine. I acknowledge The Agreement has been

negotiated fairly and Buyer has not taken advantage of me or my current situation.

_____ **17. BUYERS KNOWLEDGE:** I understand that Buyer purchases and sells real estate as a business and that Joe Smith is a licensed real estate salesperson in the state of Rhode Island

_____ **18. NO PRECLUDING AILMENTS:** I have no physical, mental or emotional

ailments that preclude me from signing The Agreement.

_____ **19. NOT UNDER THE INFLUENCE:** I am not now under the influence of

alcohol or any other mind-altering substance, nor am I taking medication that would cloud

my judgment or make me unable to think clearly.

_____ **20. NO OTHER PROMISES:** I have not been promised anything other than

what is described in The Agreement. There are no unresolved issues, no "side agreements,"

nor are there other terms not disclosed in The Agreement.

To get the forms discussed in this book and an additional free gift, visit www.fastcashforms.com

_____ **21. NOT UNDER DURESS:** I am not under duress and have signed The

Agreement of my own free will, without any undue financial pressure. I have signed of my

own free will and Buyer has in no way pressured me into signing The Agreement.

_____ **22. FULLY SATISFIED WITH AGREEMENT:** I am fully satisfied with all

terms and conditions contained in The Agreement.

Dated this _____ day of _____, 20_____.

* _____ *
_____

     Seller (Signature)   Seller (Signature)

To get the forms discussed in this book and an additional free gift, visit www.fastcashforms.com

Property Information Sheet

Address	_____	Date	_____
City	_____ State ____	Zip	_____

Owner Information

Owner 1	_____	SS#	_____
Driver's Lic	_____		
Address	_____		
City	_____ State ____	Zip	_____

Home Phone	_____	Work Phone	_____
Cell Phone	_____	Fax	_____
Email	_____		

Owner 2	_____	SS#	_____
Driver's Lic	_____		
Address	_____		
City	_____ State ____	Zip	_____

Home Phone	_____	Work Phone	_____
Cell Phone	_____	Fax	_____
Email	_____		

Comments

To get the forms discussed in this book and an additional free gift, visit www.fastcashforms.com

Mortgage Information

Mortgage Company	
Loan Number	
Contact Name	
Address	City
State	Zip
Phone	Fax
Mortgage Company	
Loan Number	
Contact Name	
Address	City
State	Zip
Phone	Fax

Owner Information

Telephone Company		Phone #	
Electric Company		Phone #	
Gas Company		Phone #	
Water/Sewer		Phone #	
Cable/DSL		Phone #	
Laundry		Phone #	
Landscaping		Phone #	
Trash Removal		Phone #	
Snow Removal		Phone #	
Maintenance		Phone #	
Attorney		Phone #	

To get the forms discussed in this book and an additional free gift, visit www.fastcashforms.com

METTING THE SELLER CHECKLIST

- Buying Packet
- Credibility Kit
- Business Cards
- Camera

BUYING PACKET CHECKLIST

- Property Information Sheet
- Inspection Checklist
- Offer Calculation Worksheet
- Purchase and Sale Agreement
- Seller's Acknowledgement Document
- Residential Seller Disclosure
- Authorization to Release Information

To get the forms discussed in this book and an additional free gift, visit www.fastcashforms.com

Chapter 8: Meeting the Homeowner

You have prepared your folder with all the documentation you need for your meeting with the seller now it's time to visit the property, build rapport with the seller and get it under agreement

Arriving at the Property

Make sure you are on time. Even if you have to leave early and park around the corner for 15 minutes, do whatever it takes to be on time. If you are late, you are sending the homeowner a message that you do not respect their time and send other negative thoughts into their head such as; if you can't even show up on time how are you going to provide a solution in time. Therefore be on time and this will be the first thing you do to separate yourself for the competition.

Drive a nice car but not a high end luxury car like a Hummer or BMW. On the other hand you do not want to drive a broken down car either. If you drive up in a beater, they will think you need more help than they do. If you show up in a luxury car they will think that you are out of their league. You want to be dressed nice by wearing business casual clothing like tan pants and a collared shirt. Be aware that they are watching you from the window and are already making subconscious decisions about whether to do business with you or not. First impressions are everything especially when you are trying to earn someone's trust. Greet them at the door with a firm handshake and give them a sincere compliment.

Getting to the Kitchen Table

When you get inside the property, they will want to invite you into the living room or family room and sit on the sofa to talk about

To get the forms discussed in this book and an additional free gift, visit www.fastcashforms.com

their situation or they will want you to tour the house. You want to do neither at first. The first thing you want to do is get them to sit down at the kitchen table. If the kitchen table is full of dishes or laundry, offer to help clear it off. Tell them you like to sit at the kitchen table or dining room table because it is easier to do business that way. Tell them you would like to sit down so that you can explain what we are going to do tonight; would that be okay?

Always ask for permission because what you are doing is gaining their trust in small steps each time they say yes. As you are telling them this, you want to take everything out of your briefcase and place it on the table. Take out the calculator, files, folders, note pad, the pen they will sign with, and anything you will need. You never want to introduce something new later in the negotiation. If you do, you may surprise them and they may be confused as to what is happening and say no. Remember a confused mind always says no. That is why you are taking everything out of your bag and then explaining what you will do while you are there.

Tell them I am going to ask you a few questions. You might ask some of the same questions as before but your goal here is to build rapport and see if their answer is consistent. Find something in common. Maybe you saw something as you entered the house that you have in common. I will then tell them a little about my company and myself and make sure you make a motion to or point to your presentation book so they know what is in the binder and will be expecting it.

Credibility Kit

If you are not using a presentation or credibility kit, you are missing out on opportunities and making the appointment with the seller more difficult than it needs to be. Throughout the entire process

To get the forms discussed in this book and an additional free gift, visit www.fastcashforms.com

from answering the phone or knocking on the door to this moment you have separated yourself from the competition. The presentation kit will separate you and help build credibility which will put the homeowner at ease. Listed below is a Checklist of everything you should have in your credibility kit.

CREDIBILITY KIT CHECKLIST

- ✓ Company Profile
- ✓ Advertisements (Laminated)
    - o Newspaper
    - o Yellow Pages
- ✓ Highlights of Background, Experience, Accreditations, and Group Memberships
- ✓ Personal Profile of Each Partner(Include Picture of Family)
- ✓ Properties you Have bought and Sold with before and after Pictures
- ✓ What you do & your Resources/Team you have to do it
- ✓ How you can Help your Clients
- ✓ Why your solution is better than what others can provide (i.e. Realtors)
- ✓ BBB Certificate
- ✓ Your Credit Score

To get the forms discussed in this book and an additional free gift, visit www.fastcashforms.com

- ✓ Character References
- ✓ Testimonials

Explaining the rest of the process

After introducing them to the creditability kit, we explain the rest of the process. Tell them we will walk around the property and then we will come back to the table and I will ask you more questions to get a handle on your situation. Then what we will do is make a decision. I'll make a decision whether or not this is something that I can work with and then you'll make a decision as to whether or not you want to work with me.

What you just accomplished is the take away close. Now they are thinking he may not want to work with us. They knew that they could decide to work with you or not but they never thought you would not want to work with them. Now that you have given them the overview as to what will happen, you want to get right into it.

Ask Questions

Review the questions that were answered from the phone interview. This will allow them to expand upon the answers and will give you the opportunity to get more information and build more rapport.

Presenting the Presentation Kit

Go through your entire presentation kit with the homeowner. This is your opportunity to build trust with them. Some of the items to highlight will be:

To get the forms discussed in this book and an additional free gift, visit www.fastcashforms.com

Member of the Better Business Bureau
Profile of yourself and any business partners
The name of your company and history
Solutions you can provide
Benefits to working with you
Testimonials from the homeowners, letter from your attorney, CPA, church or Community organizations

After you go through the presentation/credibility kit the homeowner will have trust in you and your ability to help them out.

Walk the Property

As they take you on the property tour be sure to take your property inspection form with you along with a plan to take notes. As you notice something wrong with the property do not bring negative attention to it. Pause and stare at the problem and take notes. Touch it or feel it but don't say how bad it is. They will usually notice you looking at it and they will offer a story of how long it has been like that and what happened. If they don't offer to explain the problem you can kindly ask what happened as you are staring at the problem.

I usually like to find something I have in common with them by looking around for things I recognize. I also like to make positive comments about the property such as it is nicely decorated, the big rooms, etc. Remember this is their home. As you're doing this, make sure you are filling out the property inspection form so that you will be able to calculate the rehab number.

To get the forms discussed in this book and an additional free gift, visit www.fastcashforms.com

PROPERTY TOUR DETAILS

The property tour should not take very long; depending on the size of the property, it should take about 10-30 minutes for the property tour. You are not looking to put together a detailed estimate on the repairs as you will do this once you have it under contract. Your goal is to tour the property and come up with an approximate rehab cost. Be sure to bring a pen and notebook. I often bring a clip board as well because I find it easier to write on than loose paper. You want to look organized and professional while you are there, so make sure you organize and gather what you will need ahead of time. The homeowner may tell you to just look around yourself. As much as you might want to be alone as you tour the property, you want to be sure to have them with you.

You will use this time together to build rapport with them. During the property tour, you will spend the most amount of time with the seller away from the kitchen table. Don't blow this chance at getting them to like you and trust you. You will hire a professional inspector after you get it under contract but make sure you spend enough time in each room to evaluate what it needs in repairs. Use the inspection checklist in order to take notes on each of the areas of the property. Let's go through the property and we will give you an idea of what you are looking for in each part of the property.

Exterior of House

As you were walking up to the house, you took a quick look at the roof, siding, gutters and landscaping. Curb appeal is what gets prospective buyers out of their car and into the property. If you have poor curb appeal, you will have trouble selling. As you walk around the house, count all the windows. It is best to count from the outside so

To get the forms discussed in this book and an additional free gift, visit www.fastcashforms.com

that you don't miss any of them. Note the type of siding and condition and look at the gutters to see if they need any repairs. If the gutters are full of leaves or are not draining properly, you may have some water intrusion in the house.

If there is a deck or patio, walk on it and note the condition. Does it feel structurally safe, does any of it need replacing or does it just need to be power washed? Open all the exterior doors you come across. Always ask the homeowner prior to opening a door. You don't know what is on the other side. Walk into the yard and walk away from the house. How does the grass look? Does it need reseeding or are there just patches that need replacing? Do you notice any covers on the ground? There are two covers you should be on the lookout for: cesspool/septic and well cover.

Just because the property is hooked up to the sewer doesn't mean there is an old septic hole on the property. Just because there are sewers in the street doesn't mean they are connected to it. Do you see any pipes sticking out of the ground? If the house is heated with oil heat, or oil was the heating fuel in the past, there could be a tank buried underground. As you make your way back to the front of the property, check out the parking situation. Is the amount of parking suitable and functioning well? Is there parking?

Interior: Floors, walls, and ceilings

A cosmetic update is usually needed in these three areas. Note the type of flooring (hardwood, ceramic, tile, vinyl flooring, laminate, or carpet) and what action you will have to take such as repair or replace. Carpet can be cleaned or replaced and a vinyl floor will need either a skim coat of leveler or a new sub floor. With hardwoods you have three options: buff/shine, sand, and refinish or rip out and replace.

To get the forms discussed in this book and an additional free gift, visit www.fastcashforms.com

What are the walls covered with? Is that paint or wallpaper or paint over wall paper? If you have not seen it yet, don't worry you will. Many people detest wall paper but they many don't strip it from the wall. They decide to paint over it hoping it will go away. The walls could be paneling as well which in most cases you will want to replace. What we find is that the paneling was either nailed or glued to the wallboard behind it. Always assume the worst that you will have to put new wall board on the walls.

Look up as you walk into each room. Do you see any stains on the ceiling? Is the texture of the ceiling flat or does it have a plaster/sand finish or one of those popcorn ceilings? If there are stains, ask the seller if they know how long the stains have been there and what might have caused them.

Interior: Doors and Closets

Open every closet and door that you find but again always ask the homeowner's permission. Inspect the doors for damage and if they close properly. The closets are good to look in because you may find mold or water damage inside.

Interior: Electric; Outlets, Switches, and Light Fixtures

As you walk from room to room, check to see if the lights work. Are there enough plugs and do the plugs have three prongs or two prongs. If there are only two holes in the outlet, the outlet is most likely not grounded. Don't be alarmed as this is very common on older construction. You will want to check with an electrical contractor to see if you need to upgrade them. As you flip the switch for the light in each room, look up at the light fixture. Is there one there? Does it need replacing? Are they outdated?

To get the forms discussed in this book and an additional free gift, visit www.fastcashforms.com

Interior: Kitchen

What is the condition of the cabinets? Do they need to be replaced or just refaced with new hardware? You can paint wood cabinets as well. What type of counter top is there and is it in good condition or does it need replacement? Look at the walls around the countertop. Do you see any GFCI (ground fault circuit interruption) outlets? Turn the water on in the sink and open the cabinet below the sink. Are the pipes leaking? Does the bottom of the cabinet looks like it has been damaged by water? Ask the homeowner which appliances they are leaving in the house. The more they leave the better. Even if the stove or refrigerator is not suitable for the house, it may work in a rental property you own or you could sell it to another landlord.

Interior: Bathroom

Look on the wall for a GFCI (ground fault circuit interruption) outlet. What is the condition of the vanity? Is it out of style? Do you need to update the mirror or light fixture? Look up on the ceiling; do you see a fan up there? Is there mold or mildew on the ceiling or walls? What condition is the tub/shower in? Does it have that pink and black 1960's tile or is the tub a color that is out of style? You have two options, replace it with a brand new one or hire a tub and tile refinisher to paint the tub or tile a better color. Does the toilet need to be replaced? Can you just replace the seat to make it look better?

Interior: Basement

Locate the electric panel. What size main breaker is in it? (60, 100, 150, or 200 amps) Does the panel have circuit breakers or fuses? How many fuses or breakers are there? What type of wire is coming out of the panel, Romex or knob and tube? If it is an old house, it may have knob and tube. Many insurance companies and building

To get the forms discussed in this book and an additional free gift, visit www.fastcashforms.com

inspectors do not like to see knob and tube in the basement. Do you see a water main or a well pump? How does it smell in the basement? Do you notice any dampness or standing water?

Is there a sump pump? Ask them how often it goes on and runs. Find the heating system and the type of fuel used and if there is a separate hot water tank. Is the heating system a steam system? Are the pipes wrapped and insulated in asbestos?

Interior: Attic and Garage

Always check the attic and garage. The attic may be full of the homeowner's belongings. Do you notice any leaks around the chimney? Open the garage door. Just because there is a garage door doesn't mean there is a garage behind it. Many people will convert this space to living space and not remove the garage door. Another reason to check the shed or garage is that they may be storing some hazardous chemicals in there.

As you make your way through the house, continue to make conversation with the homeowner. You are looking for common ground. You may notice that they have a hobby or interest in something. In between taking notes, take a minute to ask them about it. You might notice some hunting equipment or fishing equipment. Try to get them to tell you stories about some of their best moments. People love to talk about themselves. The more they talk about the things they enjoy the happier they will become.

Property Tour Conclusion

The outcome of the property tour is that you should now have a better idea of the condition of the property. Use the information that you gathered to estimate a rehab number. Remember you will have

To get the forms discussed in this book and an additional free gift, visit www.fastcashforms.com

your contractors and an inspector come in to view the property after you get it under contract.

When you first start, you may consider taking a general contractor with you to get a better idea of the cost of repairs. You will want to start to estimate what some of the costs are for certain repairs so you can have a system whether it is by the room or for individual repairs. Always add a 20% buffer to your rehab numbers as that will give you a cushion if things don't go as expected or you uncover additional information after you close.

Getting the Agreement Signed

Getting the Purchase and Sales agreement Signed is your ultimate goal of your visit. After you complete your property Tour, you may ask the homeowners for a few minutes so that you can do a rough calculation of the rehab. Once you are done your calculations you want to compare the number you calculated with the original number you came up with to see how your Maximum Allowable Offer is affected. Most of the time it will go down since you will find more repairs then the seller mentioned on the phone.

Once you determine you maximum you can pay, you want to get the seller back to the kitchen table to present your offer and get agreement on price and terms from the seller. Once this is accomplished, then you want to get the Purchase and Sales Agreement, Authorization to Release Information (if necessary), seller's disclosures, and seller's acknowledgement signed. In addition, you want to get any other documents you can such as an existing survey

To get the forms discussed in this book and an additional free gift, visit www.fastcashforms.com

PROPERTY INSPECTION CHECKLIST

Property Inspection Checklist

ADDRESS:		DATE:	
EXTERIOR COSTS			
Items	Work Needed		Cost
Roof/Gutters			
Windows			
Siding			
Doors			
Electric Wire			
Bulkhead			
Deck			
Paint			
Driveway			
Garage			
Well/City H2O			
Sewer/Septic			
Landscaping			
Misc			
	TOTAL EXTERIOR COST		
Exterior Checklist	Standing Water Neighbors Grade of Land Undergropund Oil Tank Foundation Height off ground		

TOTAL REHAB COST

Exterior	
Interior	
20% Rehab Buffer	
TOTAL REHAB COST	

To get the forms discussed in this book and an additional free gift, visit www.fastcashforms.com

Property Inspection Checklist

INTERIOR NOTES

Room	Work Needed	Cost
Living Room		
Dining Room		
Kitchen		
Hallway Dwn		
Bath Down		
Hallway Up		
Bath Up		
Bed 1		
Bed 2		
Bed 3		
Basement		
Basement Checklist	Finished Furnace Type Oil Tank Leak Hot water tank (rented?) Electric Type Foundation Type Structure Termites Wet Mold Sump pump Asbestos	

COMMON COSTS

Sheetrock		
Paint		
Doors		
Light Fixtures		
Flooring		
Electric		
Plumbing		
Heating		
DEMO		
Clean out		
MISC		
TOTAL INTERIOR COST		

To get the forms discussed in this book and an additional free gift, visit www.fastcashforms.com

How to Use Interior Checklist

Input all Notes in Top Section for each room but add common items cost in common area. (i.e for kitchen cabinets: put notes for cabinet replacement under kitchen "upodates needed" cell and put cost for cabinets in kitchen cost cell. If a common item like a door needs replacement in the kitchen, put notes under the kitchen notes section like "1 door needs replacement" then add 1 door to the total number of doors that need to replaced under the Common Cost Breakdown section.

To get the forms discussed in this book and an additional free gift, visit www.fastcashforms.com

Chapter 9: Due Diligence

Congratulations, now you have gotten the property under agreement. Before going to the property you determined your ARV by looking at the listing sheets of all the properties that had sold and while you were at the property you approximated how much the rehab will cost. Now that you have the property locked up under contract it now makes sense to spend more time evaluating the property to verify the accuracy of your preliminary analysis.

This is called "Due Diligence" and you will conduct this detailed due diligence during your inspection period so you can determine if you want to move forward with the purchase of the property. You will be evaluating the comparables, , the location of the subject property, the neighbors, the neighborhood, your inspection and rehab accuracy, and the title.

Checking out your Competition

How does the subject property compare to the other properties listed for sale? Will your listing price be above, below, or equal to the comps? You want to be either the same price as your competition or less. In most cases the subject property will be in better condition than the comps because after you purchase the property, you will rehab and update it. What you want to do is, drive past some or all of the comps. Get a feel for the neighborhood. Do the comps look better or worse than they did on paper?

Location Evaluation

As you drive through the neighborhood, look at the types and quality of the houses. (Ranch, Cape, Colonial, Contemporary)? Is the

To get the forms discussed in this book and an additional free gift, visit www.fastcashforms.com

subject property the largest house in the neighborhood, average, or the smallest? Is the neighborhood an entry level house area or mid level or high end? Does your subject property match? Location and neighborhood will play a large key in determining the sales ability of a property. Whether you are familiar with the area or not, you need to understand why other people would want to live here. What school district is the subject property in? Is the property in the middle of the woods or hard to find? Is the subject property surrounded by other residential houses or are there commercial or industrial buildings nearby?

You have made your way around the neighborhood and have a better feel for it. As you turn down the street that the subject property is on, start to look at the houses immediately surrounding the property. How does the curb appeal compare to the others? By now you have confirmed your comps and have a more solid idea in regards to property value.

Property Evaluation Tips

If you didn't go to the property around dinner time (5-6pm) you should revisit the property around this time. This is when traffic will be high from everyone returning from work and more people are on the streets. Another good time is when it starts to get dark to get a good feel for what type of neighborhood the subject property is in. When you get out of your car, the first thing you want to do is close your mouth and open your ears. The sounds you are hearing are the same sounds a buyer will hear when they come to buy the house from you. In most cases your buyer will be visiting the homeowner later in the day as people are coming home or going back out.

As you are listening to the background noise, take note of anything that is out of the ordinary or could make the property more

To get the forms discussed in this book and an additional free gift, visit www.fastcashforms.com

challenging to sell such as traffic, a train going by, the neighbor's vicious dogs are barking next door, or just a lot of people hanging around near the property. You want to find these things out before you buy the property to know if you will have to adjust your ARV.

Verifying Accuracy of your Inspection and Rehab

Hire a qualified home inspector to inspect the property. The money you spend here is minor compared to what it might cost you if you don't have an inspection. The inspection will also provide you a list of items that need attention. Make a list of each of the areas the inspector was concerned with and develop a scope of work for your contractors. A scope of work is a detailed summary of work to be performed and what materials will be used.

Provide this scope of work to your contractors so they can prepare an accurate bid. You will want two or three bids for most of the work that needs to be done as the price will vary significantly from contractor to contractor. Now is to find out any problems with the property so either can renegotiate after your findings or back out of the deal if then numbers no longer work because your rehab is going to cost a lot more than you originally thought.

Verifying Good Title

Another thing you are going to do is to verify that the property has a clean marketable title. This way you won't run into selling the property to your buyer once your rehab is complete. You don't have to do much for this. All you need to do is ask the attorney to start a full title search once you have the property under contract and have done some of your initial due diligence. We will discuss this in more detail in the "Closing the Deal" chapter where we go over step by step what you need to do to close on the property once you have it under contract.

To get the forms discussed in this book and an additional free gift, visit www.fastcashforms.com

Chapter 10: Buying "CASH"

As you get into the quick turn real estate business, you will find the word "CASH" used in many cases. The reason investors use the word "CASH" is because it means fast. It is saying that I as the buyer do not need to go to the bank and qualify for financing. After all, besides clear title, financing is usually what holds up the sale of real estate from happening more quickly. Sellers need a fast solution with no mortgage contingency in most cases and there are several benefits to buying with cash:

>Clearest and easiest way to buy quickly:
>No bank fees
>No bank qualifying
>No attachments to the seller
>Less paperwork
>Less confusing to the seller
>Full control of the property

WHERE YOU GET THE CASH

You may be thinking this all sounds great but I don't have enough cash to buy a property. We did not say it needed to be your cash. Whenever you can, you want to be using other people's money or OPM. There are many methods to obtain the money and you may already have the cash and don't even realize it. Here are some of the common sources.

To get the forms discussed in this book and an additional free gift, visit www.fastcashforms.com

Line of Credit

Definition: Money borrowed from a lending institution that is unsecured. Unsecured means you don't have to pledge any collateral to get the money. It is like a credit card but the advantage is that you access to the money with checks. The advantage of using a line of credit over getting a loan is that you have access to the money but only have to pay interest on it as you use it. You can use this money for rehab, down payment money, and purchase of property.

Partners

Definition: Form a partnership where one person brings the money and the other brings the deal and you split the profits 50/50. In some cases the split will be different, but don't get greedy. When forming a partnership be sure to enter into an agreement so that all parties involved will know from the start how the partnership will operate, how profits will be split and finally the breakup plan. Always plan for the divorce and put it in writing. It will avoid all sorts of problems should the partnership end prematurely due to a death, disability of a member, partner wanting to end it, or an unresolved dispute. This is a good way to find money when you start out, but this will be the most expensive form of OPM.

Credit Cards

You can obtain a cash advance from a credit card. Try to find credit cards with the lowest interest rates and without reoccurring fees. Some credit card companies will charge a fee bases on the amount of the cash advance and some will have a minimum fee or no fee at all.

To get the forms discussed in this book and an additional free gift, visit www.fastcashforms.com

Home Equity: Line of Credit

This source will allow you to access the equity in a property. Keep in mind it can be your primary residence, a vacation home, or investment property. We suggest when you use this method; do not borrow more that 80% of the value of the property. As you get over the 80% loan to value, you will begin to create a problem for yourself if the market moves in a negative direction or you find yourself in need of money for some other reason. You will have left yourself with no emergency money. When it comes to this source of money, you will have to choose; get all the money up front as a lump sum and your payments will be principle and interest, or you can get access to a line of credit that is collateralized by some real estate and you will only take the money as you need it and will be required to pay interest payments only.

The one that you want is the line of credit, not the loan. The line will allow you to pay interest on the part that you are using and not to the entire amount. Your payments will also be reduced since you do not have to pay back principle. In addition, you can pay back any or all of the principle at anytime without penalty and then have access to that principle immediately.

Hard Money

Hard money lenders are either people that have money to lend as a business or they are money brokers to high net worth individuals or others who have money to lend. You will find them in a variety of places but some of the key places are newspaper classifieds under "money to lend", referrals from you local Real Estate Investment Association (REIA), or mortgage brokers. The typical terms a hard money lender charges 3-6 points (1 point =1% of the loan) amount and 14-16% interest.

To get the forms discussed in this book and an additional free gift, visit www.fastcashforms.com

They will usually lend about 65% of the value of the property and some have programs where they can go higher up to 100'% loan to value. You may use them to obtain the money to purchase the property and or the rehab part of the project. Yes, the interest rates are high but hard money is still less expensive than a partner. Besides you are just factoring it into the deal so it doesn't matter how much they charge as long as you factor it into the deal and you are making money.

Private Money

By far this is the best source of OPM. The people who are private money lenders are normal people just like you. They have money invested in stocks, bonds, mutual funds, savings accounts, and CD'S and are looking for a higher rate of return in their money. The typical terms are no points and 10-12% interest. 10-12% is just a guide; you could pay less depending upon the person.

The people who need payments will get 10% and those who are willing and able to wait until the property is sold to get the interest plus their money back will get the 12%. They will usually lend 70-80% of the after repaired value of the property. They can provide a first mortgage or second or third mortgage. This money is secured by the property because you will sign a promissory note and a mortgage.

They will be named on your property insurance policy as an additional insured or mortgagee and they will get the lenders title insurance policy. Private lenders are all around you. Anyone with money is a potential private lender. You will have to network to find them. Tell people what you are doing and how you are doing it. When you talk to someone about being a private money lender, you must tell

To get the forms discussed in this book and an additional free gift, visit www.fastcashforms.com

them about the opportunity instead of being in a position of asking out of need.

Why Seller wants to know you are using CASH

When you are able to remove the financing contingency from a contract with the seller, you are removing a possible roadblock in their mind. They need someone who can make their situation go away. If you are not relying on bank financing, they have one more reason to choose to sell to you. Remember you are not telling them it is your cash, and in fact, you may borrow the money to buy the property; however, you are not making the deal contingent on it.

There are several other advantages for the seller if you are buying with cash and closing quickly:

- The mortgage is paid off
- No foreclosure on their record
- Fast closing
- Easiest paperwork
- Clean break from the property

There are three primary ways to purchase the property in quick turn real estate, cash or taking over the property subject to the existing mortgage staying in place commonly referred to as "subject to", and lease option. You might choose to use "Subject to" and" Lease Option" since they might require less equity and could provide the seller with a faster solution to their problems. The following chapters will provide details of how to use these methods.

To get the forms discussed in this book and an additional free gift, visit www.fastcashforms.com

Chapter 11: Buying "Subject To"

"Subject to" is when you take title or ownership of the property but leave the seller's existing mortgage in place. The loan is NOT assumed by a new buyer but instead the mortgage remains in the seller's name while the deed is transferred to you or your entity. A majority of the mortgages have a clause in them called the "due upon sale clause". Taking over the mortgage may be considered bank fraud because the clause says that upon the transfer or sale or assignment of beneficial interest, the loan must be paid in full. The homeowner will be at least in violation of the mortgage they signed and some states consider the practice of convincing a seller to do this unlawful. The concealment of the fact that the due upon sale clause has been triggered is what is illegal or against the law.

The mortgage industry is regulated by the federal government and the violation will be a matter of federal law. You also have to consider several state statues as well as common law. These violations will be civil not criminal but again you are in violation of the law. There will be many that will tell you there is a way around the due upon sale clause but there simply is not.

One way to avoid the due upon sale clause is to not transfer the property until the sale takes place and the mortgage is paid off. You can accomplish the same results as "subject to" by doing a lease option. After all the benefits to buying on lease option are the same as buying "subject to" and they are:

> No Bank Fees
> No Bank Qualifying
> Much Less out of Pocket Costs
> Quick Closing

To get the forms discussed in this book and an additional free gift, visit www.fastcashforms.com

Chapter 12: Buying Lease Option

Buying through a lease option will be the other purchase strategy we can use. A lease option is a good option for you since it could require that you come up with less money to close. Homeowners will be inclined to do a lease option because this can happen as fast as or faster than paying cash for the property. They may get some equity now and the rest when the property is sold.

The damage to their credit score will be potentially reduced since you saved them from foreclosure, made up their back payments, and are now making on time payments that will be reflected on their credit report.

Why would a Seller do a Lease Option with you?

>Stop Foreclosure Auction fast
>Lessen the damage to their credit score
>Quick process
>Quick Solution to their problems
>Money today

Properties in Foreclosure require additional steps when doing a lease option so we are going to focus on this type of motivated seller when we go through the process. IF you have a homeowner not in foreclosure you can just reduce the amount of steps. In most cases the homeowner in foreclosure will be behind on their mortgage payments. In order to stop the foreclosure auction one of two things needs to happen.

To get the forms discussed in this book and an additional free gift, visit www.fastcashforms.com

Either the mortgage needs to be paid off in full by you paying cash for the property or making the loan current by making up the back payments and attorney's fees by doing a lease option.

In order to make the loan current you will need to make up the back payments to stop the auction. Do not make the loan current or pay any money until the homeowner has vacated the property. If you solve their problem before they leave, they won't have any reason to go. The following are the steps in the process:

1. Meet with the seller (1st meeting)
2. Contact Mortgage Company
3. Have title checked
4. 2nd Meeting with seller
5. 3rd Meeting with seller
6. Stop foreclosure auction
7. Make monthly payments
8. Market property to find buyer
9. Sell to Buyer

Meet with Seller

This is the first meeting that you have with them to determine if you have a deal. Prior to arriving, you either knew that they wanted to sell or during your first meeting all other options were eliminated and the homeowner decided to sell the property. During this meeting you will obtain the following documents:

Authorization to Release Information
Property Information Sheet
Offer Calculation Worksheet
Purchase and Sales Agreement

To get the forms discussed in this book and an additional free gift, visit www.fastcashforms.com

During the first meeting you may not have determined if you will buy for cash or buy on Lease Option. In most cases you will need more information to make that determination. The authorization to release information will allow you to obtain a loan pay off amount and how much will be needed to bring the mortgage current and stop the foreclosure sale.

You will need a purchase and sales agreement because you plan on buying the property unless your inspection or due diligence provides information that shows you not to buy it. If you are going to buy using the lease option strategy, you will discuss the details regarding how it works in the 2nd meeting you have with the seller. Prior to meeting with the seller for the second meeting, you will want to have your title company check the title and make sure it is in order.

2nd Meeting with the Seller

After you get the numbers from the bank, the title comes back in order, you have had the property inspected, contractors have submitted quotes for work to be done, and you have determined it's a deal, it is time to set up the second meeting. At the second meeting the following documents need to be signed.

> Warranty Deed
> Insurance Company Letter
> Lease Agreement
> Option to Purchase Agreement
> Performance Mortgage

Even though you are entering into two separate agreements with the seller, one to lease the property and another to have the option to purchase the property at a later date, you need to get the warranty deed

To get the forms discussed in this book and an additional free gift, visit www.fastcashforms.com

signed now. The warranty deed will be held in escrow by your attorney with instructions as to when it should be recorded. The reason you need to get the deed signed now is that you may have trouble finding the seller later when it comes time to execute the purchase of the property. This way you can have all the paper work for the sale filled out ahead of time and the seller won't have to do much when it comes time to execute the option to purchase.

Since you will be leasing the property from the seller, the ownership and property insurance will remain in the seller's name. You will instruct the seller to contact their insurance company and inform them that they have rented the property and are no longer occupying the property and to update the insurance policy to reflect it is a non owner occupied property and that it is vacant.

Lease Agreement

This will be the agreement between you and the seller and will describe that you will be leasing for a period of X years for monthly rent. The monthly rent will usually be equal to the seller's mortgage payment, taxes, and insurance. An example of a lease agreement is included on the next page however you should consult an attorney in the state you are doing business in to make sure the document meets the laws of the state.

Option Agreement

This will be the agreement between you and the seller that gives you the right to purchase the property at a later date for a price determined today. There will be an option consideration component to this agreement and you will want that to be as little as possible. If you are making up back payments and bringing the seller's mortgage current, your option consideration fee will be the amount to bring the

To get the forms discussed in this book and an additional free gift, visit www.fastcashforms.com

loan current. An example of an option agreement is included on the next page however you should consult an attorney in the state you are doing business in to make sure the document meets the laws of the state.

Performance Mortgage

A Performance Mortgage is a mortgage or deed of trust that is used as a security instrument to secure an obligation of one party of an agreement. Essentially you obtain the rights of a second mortgage. The mortgage in this case is not securing the promise to repay a sum of money but is securing the promise to abide by the terms of the option agreement you entered into. This technique puts you in a much better position from a priority of liens standpoint.

The primary difference between the mortgage or deed of trust and a performance mortgage is that you replace Lender (Grantor) and Borrower (Grantee) with Obligor and Obligee respectively. In order to use this technique you must contact a real estate attorney and have them draft a performance mortgage that complies with the laws of your state.

3rd Meeting with the Seller

The third meeting will take place after the seller moves out of the property and has removed all personal belongings. If the seller is getting any money, it is given at this point. You will now make the mortgage current because the seller has moved out and the lease and option are in effect.

To get the forms discussed in this book and an additional free gift, visit www.fastcashforms.com

What happens after the 3rd meeting?

After the third meeting you will complete all repairs to the property to get it sold. During the time you are making monthly payments, make sure you are not paying the seller. You want to make all payments directly to the mortgage company. If you pay the seller, they may not make the payment and they will be right back in the same situation. If you pay the seller, they may not make the payment and they will be right back in the same situation.

If the seller is concerned that you are not going to make the payments, you can set up an escrow account with an attorney or escrow company to make the payments for you. Give permission to the seller to check on the escrow account to make certain that the payment is being made.

To get the forms discussed in this book and an additional free gift, visit www.fastcashforms.com

LEASE AGREEMENT

_____ (hereinafter referred to as "Tenant", the amount of $_____, as evidenced by check,
as a deposit which, upon acceptance of this Lease Agreement, shall belong to the Owner of the premises and/or it's agent, (hereinafter referred to as Owner"), and shall be applied to the due amount only, as follows:

    Total Monthly Rent:
    $_____

Tenant hereby offers to rent from the Owner the premises whose legal address is

_____

TERM:
    The term hereof shall commence on_____, terminating on_____ For a total consideration of _____ which shall be due and payable on the _____ day of _____, and continuing thereafter in accordance with the terms and conditions of this lease.

Tenant will have access to home on by giving the owner a twenty four hour notice to show the property to prospective tenants/buyers or Contractors. Owner agrees to give Tenant access prior to taking possession of the property once properly notified.

To get the forms discussed in this book and an additional free gift, visit www.fastcashforms.com

RENT:
> Owner agrees to continue to carry homeowners insurance on this home and to have the policy changed to a non-owner occupied insurance policy.

UTILITY BILLS

> Tenant agrees and shall be responsible for the payment of all utilities, Tenant shall make arrangement at his/her expense to initiate service of utilities, including to electric, gas, no later
than the first day of tenancy, and shall pay the utility expense in a timely fashion.

ASSIGNMENT AND SUBLETTING

Tenant may assign this agreement to another party, but is still responsible to the owner per this rental agreement. Resident refers to the person(s) occupying the property.

ENTRY AND INSPECTION

> Tenant shall permit Owner or Owner's agent to enter the premises at reasonable times and upon reasonable notice for the purpose of inspecting the premises.

> All entry to the property must be made through the tenant.
The tenant can then notify the resident and arrange an appointment convenient for all parties. Landlord agrees not to call, stop by, or visit residents without the tenants consent. Consent cannot unreasonably be withheld. This is for the liability protection of both the tenant and the Landlord.

To get the forms discussed in this book and an additional free gift, visit www.fastcashforms.com

MAINTENANCE, REPAIRS OR ALTERATIONS

The Landlord gives the tenant the right to make repairs/improvements to the property at the tenants expense. All repairs will be done by the tenants contractors unless otherwise specified.

All repairs, major and minor will be the responsibility of the tenant-except the first 60 days of this agreement, which shall
be the full responsibility of the Landlord.

Landlord agrees to use their homeowner's insurance to cover any items/repairs/damage that would be covered under their policy (i.e. storm damage, etc)-since tenant can't utilize their insurance for these type of repairs. Should the property become uninhabitable at any point during the lease period, the tenant will
 be released from all rent liabilities until the property is habitable
and is re-let. The amount of time that the home is uninhabitable will be the time period that will be added to the attached option agreement, rental agreement and purchase agreement. (i.e. if the home is damaged for 4 months then the option period will be
 extended for 4 months also)

NOTICES

Any notice which party may or is required to give, may be given by first class mail.

To get the forms discussed in this book and an additional free gift, visit www.fastcashforms.com

The Owner or Agent's name and address for receipt of communication pursuant to the above is:_____

LEAD PAINT

"Housing built before 1978 may contain lead-based paid. Lead paint, paint chips and dust can cause health hazards if not managed properly. Lead exposure is especially harmful to young children and pregnant women. Before renting pre-1978 housing, owners must disclose the presence of lead based paint hazards in the dwelling. Renters must also receive a federally approved pamphlet on lead poisoning prevention."

HOLDING OVER

Any holding over after expiration hereof, unless otherwise agreed, shall be construed as a month-to-month tenancy in accordance with the terms hereof as applicable.

_____
_____
Tenant   Landlord

_____
_____
Tenant   Landlord

To get the forms discussed in this book and an additional free gift, visit www.fastcashforms.com

OPTION TO PURCHASE AGREEMENT

This Option to Purchase Agreement is made on _____ Date between

_____
(the "Seller") and

_____
(the "Buyer").

WHEREAS, Seller is the fee owner of certain real property situated in _____ County, _____, such real property having a street address of _____

_____ (the "Property").

FOR and in consideration of the covenants and obligations contained herein and other good and valuable consideration, the receipt and sufficiency of which is hereby acknowledged, Seller hereby grants to Buyer an exclusive option to purchase the aforementioned "Property." The parties hereto hereby agree as follows:

1. **OPTION TERM**. The option to purchase period commences on _____ (Date) and expires on _____ (Date).

2. **NOTICE REQUIRED TO EXERCISE OPTION**. To exercise the Option to Purchase, the Buyer must deliver to the Seller written notice of Buyer's intent to purchase.

3. **OPTION CONSIDERATION**. As consideration for this Option to Purchase Agreement, the Buyer shall pay the Seller a non-refundable fee of $_____, receipt of which is hereby acknowledged by the Seller. This amount shall be credited to the purchase price at closing if the Buyer timely exercises the option to purchase.

4. **PURCHASE PRICE**. The total purchase price for the Property is

To get the forms discussed in this book and an additional free gift, visit www.fastcashforms.com

5. **EXCLUSIVITY OF OPTION**. This Option to Purchase Agreement is exclusive

6. **CLOSING AND SETTLEMENT**. Buyer shall determine the title company at which settlement shall occur and shall inform Seller of this location in writing.

SELLER:

Sign: _____

Date: _____

Sign: _____

Date: _____

BUYER

Sign: _____

Date: _____

Sign: _____

Date: _____

To get the forms discussed in this book and an additional free gift, visit www.fastcashforms.com

REQUEST TO CANCEL INSURANCE

Insured by:_____
      Phone#:_____

Policy#:_____
      Address:_____

Mortgage Company:_____
_____
Address:_____
_____

Loan#:_____
_____

To Whom It May Concern:

Please convert my/our insurance policy to a vacant house policy at this time.

Thank you in advance,

_____
Signature   Signature

_____
Print Name   Print Name

To get the forms discussed in this book and an additional free gift, visit www.fastcashforms.com

NOTICE OF REAL ESTATE OPTION AGREEMENT
STATE OF _____ COUNTY OF _____

AN OPTION AGREEMENT has been made and entered into this _____ day of _____, 20____, between _____, as party of the first part, hereinafter referred to as "Optionor", and _____, as the party of the second part, hereinafter referred to as "Optionee" (the words Optionor and Optionee to include their respective heirs, successors and assigns where the context requires or permits).

WITNESSETH THAT: Optionor, for and in consideration of the sum of one dollar ($1.00) and other good and valuable considerations in hand paid at and before the sealing and delivery of these presents, the receipt and sufficiency whereof is hereby acknowledged, by these presents does hereby sell, convey and transfer unto said Optionee, an Option for the Sale and Purchase of the real property which is described as follows:

(Insert Legal Description)
THIS OPTION AGREEMENT PROHIBITS ADDITIONAL INDEBTEDNESS

The closing of the sale and purchase of said real property is to take place pursuant to the terms of the Agreement(s) entered into of even date herewith. Any interested party may contact:

_____, whose mailing address is _____, and whose telephone number is (_____)_____.

Should said Option Agreement fail to close for any reason and should Optionee elect not to pursue specific performance under the terms of said Agreement(s), this Notice shall be released upon the repayment to Optionee of any funds expended by Optionee in order to pay any underlying indebtedness, taxes, assessments or fees which may have been due from Optionor, plus interest.

IN WITNESS WHEREOF, the parties hereto have signed and sealed this memorandum, the day and year first above written.

To get the forms discussed in this book and an additional free gift, visit www.fastcashforms.com

S_____(
_____
Witness   **Optionor**

_____
_____
Witness   **Optionee:**

_____
Notary Public

signed, sealed, and delivered in the presence of:

To get the forms discussed in this book and an additional free gift, visit www.fastcashforms.com

Chapter 13: Closing the Deal

Closing the deal can be one of the most exciting parts of this business. It can also be the most frustrating. This part of the process is all about the details. There is a lot that can go right and a lot that can go wrong. Some deals you close will have little or no problems while others will take a lot of time and a lot of negotiations to get the deal done. You must remain in control at all times and lead the seller to the closing table.

The key word in that last sentence is "lead". If you drag them or force them to the closing table, is that a win/win situation? If someone does not want to do business with you, reason with them to change their mind but never force them. If they don't trust you, then I don't want to do business with them. They will just cause you problems after the closing primarily because it was not a win/win deal.

12 STEPS TO CLOSING

STEP 1: Contact your Attorney or Title Company

After you get the purchase and sales agreement signed by the seller, you must send it to your attorney or title company along with the earnest money deposit. Ask the attorney to start a full title search. If there is anything special about this deal or something that you are aware of that will make this a challenging closing, bring it to the attorney's attention right from the start. Something special about the deal might be that the closing is set for ten days from now or you need assistance stopping the foreclosure auction.

To get the forms discussed in this book and an additional free gift, visit www.fastcashforms.com

Other challenging items might include sellers that are divorced or separated and can't be in the same room as one another. Maybe there are a large amount of liens on the property that the seller would like to negotiate after the closing occurs. The more information and detail the closing agent or closing attorney has, the smoother the closing will go.

STEP 2: Contact the Seller's Lender (do this step when behind on payments or your purchase price is close to what they owe)

During your meeting with the seller you had them fill out and sign an authorization to release information. Call the phone number for the lender and tell them you have an authorization to release form that you would like to fax over. Ask for the fax number and fax it to them. If the file is in loss mitigation, ask for the name and extension of the person assigned to the file. You normally must wait at least 24 hours for it to be updated in their computer system. Once it is part of the file, you can then call back and get information from the seller's lender.

Getting the Payoff (do this step when behind on payments or your purchase price is close to what they owe)

Ask the lender for a payoff if you are buying the property. If you are doing a lease option you would want the payoff as well as the amount to bring the loan current. It is important to obtain the payoff since in some cases the seller thought they owed less. The payoff figure will start to rise quickly after the seller has missed several payments and the lender has gotten an attorney involved. On the average foreclosure, the attorney's fees, advertising and other fees the lender charge can quickly add up in excess of $10,000. By completing this step early in the process, you will know if you can purchase the property for the price on the purchase and sales.

To get the forms discussed in this book and an additional free gift, visit www.fastcashforms.com

If the payoff number is higher than what the homeowner thought it was, you must contact them and have another meeting. In many cases the payoff will be more than the homeowner thought but less than the purchase price, but the seller may now be getting less cash at closing and may not be happy. Don't wait until you get to the closing table to break the news to them. Have a meeting and explain what the payoff is and why it is higher and make sure they understand they will be getting less than they thought at the closing. If they are not happy or want to back out of the deal, you have two choices. Renegotiate and raise your purchase price to a level that makes them happy or try to enforce the contract as is.

If you are unable to convince them to abide by the original terms of the contract and are not successful in renegotiating, you may have to walk from the deal. Yes, you have an enforceable contract but it will not be worth going through the process to enforce it and in most cases there will not be enough time. You will have to re-evaluate the deal and see if there are some other options where you can help the homeowner out of their situation and still profit. If the payoff is about what was expected, be sure to send the payoff to the closing agent.

STEP 3: Arranging Financing

Whether you are paying cash, getting private money, hard money, or conventional financing, you need to start making financing arrangements right from day one of the contract.

Cash

If you will be using cash to close the deal, have a plan for how long it will take you to transfer the money to the closing agent if the cash is not in an account that you have quick access to. The money might be in a CD or a stock account or a self directed IRA. Make sure

To get the forms discussed in this book and an additional free gift, visit www.fastcashforms.com

you know your timeline and the timeline of the institution that has your money.

Private Money Loan/Hard Money Loan

If you are going to use private money, you will need to create a prospectus of the property to show to your private lenders. The prospectus should outline the property features, the terms, the amount you are looking for, the repairs that need to be completed, and comparable properties. Depending on the lender, you will also have to budget time to speak with them about the deal.

Some will require that they drive by the property and others will want to get inside. They will also want to know what lien holder position they will be in, if it is a first mortgage or a second, or third. Especially when there will be multiple mortgages, make sure they know what the loan to value the property will be at after they loan the money. In essence they want to know how much equity remains in case they need to foreclose.

One reason you might have multiple mortgages is that you might use one lender to fund the purchase and another to fund the rehab.

Conventional Financing

If you plan to use conventional bank financing you need to have more time to close in most cases. The trick to speeding things up with a lender is to get them involved right from the start. Make sure that you have gotten at least a pre-qualified letter. Your lender may have even gone the extra step to pre-approve you. Discuss with your lender how you can speed up the process.

To get the forms discussed in this book and an additional free gift, visit www.fastcashforms.com

Ask the mortgage broker what they will need from you in order to send the package to the underwriter. Prepare the package of information they have requested and get it back to them. Since you will get them involved from the start, you should know pretty early in the process if they can fund the deal or not. The lender usually needs four primary items: Purchase and Sales Agreement, 40 year title report, appraisal of the property, all your information such as bank statements, and tax returns. Of the four items, you are in complete control of only two and you will only have a small amount of influence or no influence over the other two.

No matter which way you get the money to do the deal, you must have a backup plan. What will you do when you get that call that says, "Sorry we are not going to be able to make the loan". If you don't have a contingency plan, you will lose out on several deals when you are under prepared.

STEP 4: Hazard Insurance

You are going to need insurance on the property unless you are buying it using a lease option. If you are using the lease option to purchase the property, the seller or lessor will need to change their policy from an owner occupied policy to a non owner occupied vacant policy. It will not take long to get the quote but start this process early. The type of insurance you want is vacant insurance combined with liability insurance.

The vacant insurance will not be inexpensive but will be the best coverage for a vacant property. Do not try and stage the house to make it look like someone is living there. You might save a few dollars but if there is a loss on the property, the insurance company will not pay and it will cost you much more in the end. Vacant insurance typically has a minimum earned component to it which means that if you get a three

To get the forms discussed in this book and an additional free gift, visit www.fastcashforms.com

month policy and it is a three month minimum earned policy, you will not get a pro-rated refund if you cancel the policy during the coverage period.

The longest term most companies offer this is one year. Most policies whether they are a 3, 6, or 12 month policy have a 3 month minimum earned component. Since you budget for six months, you should get a six month policy and will get a refund for any time over three months that you did not use. If you are using private, hard or conventional money to purchase the property, you need to add the lender's name to the insurance policy. Make sure that the amount of the coverage is at least equal to the total amount of loans on the property.

STEP 5: Property Inspection and Contractors

Schedule the property inspection for a date just after you confirm the payoff amount and that there are no title problems that will prevent you from purchasing the property. Hire a qualified home inspector to inspect the property. The money you spend here is minor compared to what it might cost you if you don't have an inspection. The inspection will also provide you a list of items that need attention. Make a list of each of the areas the inspector was concerned with and develop a scope of work for your contractors. A scope of work is a detailed summary of work to be performed and what materials will be used.

Provide this scope of work to your contractors so they can prepare an accurate bid. You will want two or three bids for most of the work that needs to be done as the price will vary significantly from contractor to contractor. After you evaluate the proposal from the contractor and have decided which contractors to use contact them and schedule a date for them to get started.

To get the forms discussed in this book and an additional free gift, visit www.fastcashforms.com

STEP 6: Check in with the Seller

During the time from when the contract was signed to the closing date, you should remain in frequent contact with the seller. If they don't hear from you they will think that something is wrong. At each step of the process, you should update them and reassure them that everything is moving along at the expected pace and you are on track for the original plan you agreed to. They need this reassurance because people will still be knocking at their door and telling them that they will pay more.

Make sure you tell the seller when you sign the purchase and sales agreement how to deal with people contacting them about their foreclosure. Tell them that if anyone calls or knocks on their door to tell them that they have solved their foreclosure problem and don't need any help; be sure to tell them not to tell the person calling or knocking how they solved their problem because it is none of their business.

This is really important because whatever information the seller provides will be used against them and used against you. If they told them they sold the house, the investor will tell them they are getting taken advantage of and they can offer them more. Avoid the whole thing by telling them that the problems have been solved and for any other details the other investor can contact the person that is representing them which is you.

Most investors will not call you but if you do, don't give them any information, just tell them the problems are behind them and to stop bothering them. The sellers are also concerned throughout the process about the contingencies in the contract. As you remove the contingencies such as title, inspection and pay off information, you

To get the forms discussed in this book and an additional free gift, visit www.fastcashforms.com

need to make them aware that the result was positive and you are getting closer.

<u>NEVER</u> allow a Seller to remain in a Property

You should also be checking with them about their job during the closing process. The only major job they have besides showing up at the closing is moving out of the property. Never allow a seller to remain in the property after you close. If you do this you are asking for trouble. To make sure that they have this process under way, make sure you ask them where they plan to go and what they are going to do with all their belongings.

Help them to find a suitable place to live. Many people under estimate the amount of time it takes to move. If they are having trouble moving or don't think they will be out before the closing, take it a step further and hire a mover for them. You can either pay for the movers yourself or pay and have them repay you from their proceeds at the closing. Whatever it takes, get them moved out because every day that goes by is costing them money and costing you too.

STEP 7: Appraisal

If you are using traditional bank financing, you will need to pay for an appraisal. The lender will select the appraiser and the appraiser will schedule an appointment with you. Be prepared to pay for the appraisal at the time you meet them at the house. When you meet the appraiser, you should bring some comps to show the value of the property. If you have a floor plan of the house, give it to them and anything else they ask for.

As the appraiser goes through the house, point out upgrades such as hardwood floors, tile, roof, windows and siding. Before the appraiser leaves, ask them what number they think the appraisal will

To get the forms discussed in this book and an additional free gift, visit www.fastcashforms.com

come in at. They may not tell you but ask them if it will come in above or below the purchase price. Be as helpful as possible to appraisers because you never know where you might see them again. Besides appraisers are a wealth of knowledge. They know areas and they know values. They also know how the banks are looking at comps and what extra information they are requiring to approve the loan. Even if you are not getting financing that requires an appraisal, you may consider having an appraisal done so you can document the "as is" value.

STEP 8: Switching over the Utilities

A week before the closing, call the utility companies and inform them that you will be buying the property on the closing date that has been set. If the seller has already moved out, make sure you tell the seller not to turn off the utilities to the property you are buying. They will have to wait until the closing for the utilities to be switched over.

This is very important because if the seller turns off the electricity prior to the closing, there may be an issue that arises at the property. One possible scenario is that the water table is on the high side and the sump pump regularly runs. Without electricity the water may back up into the basement and cause damage. We are sure you can think of some other potential problems. Another problem exists as well if the utilities are turned off prior to you switching them over, it could take several days or a week to schedule the utility company to come back and turn it on.

STEP 9: The Final Walkthrough

The day before the closing you will go to the property to see the condition and make sure that the seller is holding up to their end of the bargain. The other reason that I do the walk through is because in the next day or so contractors will be starting work on the property. Meet

To get the forms discussed in this book and an additional free gift, visit www.fastcashforms.com

the contractors that will be starting right away to answer any questions, show them the property vacant, and confirm they are ready to start the work. If you skip this step you will be sorry. If you wait until after you close to see what you bought, you will have a problem eventually.

It may be big like a house filled with mold because a pipe broke and no one was living there for a few days. In regards to water, as soon as the seller is no longer living in the property, make sure the water is turned off at the main valve inside the house.

STEP 10: The Settlement Statement

The day before the closing you should receive a preliminary settlement statement from the closing agent. Attempt to get this as many days prior to the closing that you can. Often times there will be mistakes on the settlement statement. If changes need to be made, it will be easier to make them prior to the closing than when everyone is sitting at the closing table. What you are looking for is an accurate total for the check you need to bring to the closing and an accurate number of what the seller should receive at closing. If your number is incorrect, correct it right away. If the seller number is a little lower than what they are expecting, you may want to deal with it and present it to them in person at the closing.

It could be several items affecting the amount of their proceeds from the sale. The payoff might have been higher than expected; there might have been some liens they didn't know about. The sewer and water bill may have been higher. If it is a major problem or the amount is significantly less, you will want to set up a meeting with the seller prior to the closing to make sure the seller understands why the amount is less and accepts what it is.

To get the forms discussed in this book and an additional free gift, visit www.fastcashforms.com

STEP 11: Wire Funds or Certified Check

After you have reviewed the settlement statement and know how much you need to bring to the closing, you need to get the money. You have two options. You can wire the money which will cost you about $50 or you can get a certified bank check which should be free depending on the type of account you have with your bank. The check will cost you about $10 if it is not free.

STEP 12: The Closing

The day has arrived to finally complete the process of buying the property. You may find that buying the property is more exciting than selling the property. You will collect your money when you sell but you really make your money when you buy. The closing agent will have you and the seller sits in a conference room and then after all the parties have arrived, the closing will begin. The first thing that happens is the closing agent will request a copy of your driver's license or some other form of identification. Even if you know the closing agent, and they have conducted several closings with you, they still need to photocopy the identification that each party provided at the time of closing.

The closing agent will provide you the final settlement statement. Check the statement for changes from the last draft you reviewed. The closing agent will explain the settlement statement to the seller first and get them to sign; then they will turn to you and explain it to you. The seller will then be asked to sign some other miscellaneous documents that pertain to post closing compliance. You will sign some of the documents as well and then the seller will sign the deed. The seller is done signing at this point. Many sellers think that they will walk out of the closing with a check for the amount of the proceeds.

To get the forms discussed in this book and an additional free gift, visit www.fastcashforms.com

After they sign the deed, ask the closing agent when the deed will be recorded. In most cases they will do it the same day. They will instruct the seller as to the time their check will be available and to come back after that time to get it. The reason the check is held is because the closing agent has to do one more check of the title to make sure it has not changed since the last time they updated the title. If the title checks out, the sellers get their check and you get the keys to your latest acquisition. Make sure you get the keys from the seller when they sign the deed so that you can get into the property as soon as the closing agent tells you the title checked out fine and your are now the owner of record.

Chapter 14: Selling Quickly

To be successful at real estate investing you must move quickly. If you don't sell quickly, you are giving up profit everyday that goes by between the day you buy and the day you sell. In a previous chapter we discussed quick turn real estate. In this chapter we will cover how to get that property sold.

Prior to buying the property you must determine your exit strategy. Will you sell to another investor, sell to a retail buyer, or hold the property for cash flow and long term investment. For the purposes of this chapter we will look at the first two options.

SELLING TO ANOTHER INVESTOR

This is the quickest way to sell the property. As a matter of fact you may not even have to buy the property; you can sell the contract that you have to another investor. This is called assigning a contract. The basic idea is you get a property under contract and then sell that contract to another investor for a fee. The fee can be anywhere from $5,000 to $20,000 or more.

You will have to make sure that you leave enough profit in the deal to make it worth it for the investor. You are the middle man and will buy cheap and sell cheap. Because you are selling so quickly, you will sacrifice some profit for time. You will make less but will also create time for yourself. When starting out you need to decide what is more important to you or what your needs are. Do you need time or do you have the time to put in to make more money.

To find the investor to wholesale to, you will look in a variety of places. Do you ever see those bandit signs on utility poles that say,

To get the forms discussed in this book and an additional free gift, visit www.fastcashforms.com

"We Buy Houses"? Call the number on the sign and determine if they are a qualified buyer. A qualified buyer is a buyer that can close quickly because they are paying cash and require no bank financing. The typical cash buyer can close in seven days or less. Another source of cash buyers will be the classified ads of the newspaper. Look under the section, "Property Wanted". There should be several ads that start off, "We Buy Houses". Call them and qualify them. Finally the third source is at your local real estate investment club or association (REIA). Go to your local real estate clubs and ask the person who runs the club who the most active real estate investors are in the clubs. You may even ask, who are the "Cash Buyers"? Introduce yourself to these folks and qualify them. Find out how quickly they can close and what and where they like to buy.

One reason to wholesale to another investor is to save time and the other reason is you may be able to make money on a property that doesn't fit your buying criteria. Maybe one of these cash buyers likes to buy in the war zones. As a beginner and even when you have some experience, you probably want to avoid owning property in the war zones. However, there are buyers that like the war zones and do most of their business there.

SELLING TO A RETAIL BUYER

This method of selling will produce the highest profits. There are two primary factors that will affect how long it takes to sell, the price compared to similar properties on the market and the condition of the property. When it comes to price you need to be competitive and depending upon what phase of the market cycle your market is in, your list price will have to be equal or lower by as much as 10% when wanting to sell quickly.

To get the forms discussed in this book and an additional free gift, visit www.fastcashforms.com

Determining the selling price for the property will have been determined at the time you did your analysis to buy and your flexibility in that price will be determined by how good of a deal you got. In this chapter we will discuss preparing the property, attracting buyers, prescreening buyers, and getting to the closing table.

When to start marketing the Property

Most foreclosure investing experts agree that you can start marketing the property the day you get it under agreement. You should have a provision in your purchase and sales agreement that allows you access to the property to show contractors, inspectors, and prospective buyers. The condition and exit strategy will determine who you can show and when. If you are trying to wholesale the property you can show it right after you sign the purchase and sales agreement. If you plan to sell to a retail buyer, you may not want to show the property until the property is in better condition.

Most retail buyers can't see the forest through the trees as they say. They may be turned off by the current condition and can't imagine what the property will look like when it is fixed up.

Guide to Selling Quickly

1. Buy the property right
2. Hold the property for less than six months
3. Price the property to sell
4. Start marketing as soon as possible
5. Build a buyers list
6. Show the property when at least 90% complete

Who will Sell the Property?

To get the forms discussed in this book and an additional free gift, visit www.fastcashforms.com

You will have two choices when it comes to listing your property. Will you sell it for sale by owner or sell it by listing with a Realtor. You can even use a system that involves doing both. Deciding on what method you use to sell your property does not start when the rehab is near completion. The method is determined before you close on the purchase of the property. If you plan your exit prior to purchasing the property, you will give yourself the best chance at selling the quickest.

Finding the right Realtors

Prior to purchasing the property, you will need to determine who besides yourself will sell the property. Start a search for a Realtor. You need to be specific when choosing a Realtor that will sell your property. The Realtor you are looking for is one of the top three Realtors in the area where your property is located. There are a few methods to finding out who the top Realtors are in the area. You can contact the local board of Realtors and ask for a ranking sheet of Realtors in the area.

If you have access to the MLS or know someone that will help you gather the information, you can find out what Realtors have sold the most properties in the neighborhood of your property. One of the other methods is to drive around the neighborhood where your property is located and look for "For Sale" signs. If there are not many, expand your search a mile or two away. You should start to see the same Realtor's sign over and over. Now just because they have a lot of listings doesn't mean that they can sell them. In most cases the top listing agents usually are top selling agents as well. After you compile a list, whether it is from the local board of Realtors or it is from the "For Sale" signs you saw in the area, you need to call them and interview them.

To get the forms discussed in this book and an additional free gift, visit www.fastcashforms.com

During the interview you want to find out if they have sold any properties recently that are comparable to yours, how long have they been an agent, and do they work on their own or do they have a team. After a brief conversation you should be able to narrow it down to two or three Realtors.

Interviewing the Realtors

Within 24 hours after you close on the property, you need to meet each of the Realtors at the property. If the house is vacant prior to your closing on it, you will do this prior to closing, If the property is occupied, it is best to wait until you own it before bringing the Realtor there. During the meeting the Realtor should be prepared to show you why they should be the one to list the property. They should give you a short presentation on who they are, what they have accomplished and how they plan to market your property.

You are looking for a Realtor that has been in business for at least two years, has recently sold properties in the same area as yours, lists and sells they types of properties that you have for sale, and has a marketing budget for selling properties. You also want them to be part of a Realtor team. This will increase your exposure to the property and give you the best chance of selling quickly. The two questions I typically ask them are: can you tell me what marketing you will use to sell my property? The second question comes after they have presented me with their CMA (Comparable Market Analysis). I ask them what the 30 day price is. In most cases they will give me a lower number than what their CMA shows.

During the meeting, tour the property with the Realtor and ask them what buyers are looking for in today's market. Ask them about upgrades or repairs that you are undecided about. You don't want to make any more improvements than you need to but you want to have

To get the forms discussed in this book and an additional free gift, visit www.fastcashforms.com

the quality of the property equal or above what the buyers are looking for. During the appointment with the Realtor, you should be gathering as much information about them and their thoughts on what repairs will be needed in order to sell quickly.

Final Selection of Realtor

After meeting with the two or three you selected to meet with, you need to decide who you feel will get the job done. In most cases, they are all qualified but you need to evaluate the whole package and make a decision. You may be tempted to go with the one that gave you the highest price but that person won't always be your best option. They may be good at getting top dollar for their listings but may take longer to do so. You need a price that will get the property under contract within 30 days. Now that you have a good idea which Realtor you will hire if you need one, it is time to get back to the other method to sell.

For Sale By Owner (FSBO)

After you finish your meetings with the Realtors you want to put a FSBO sign in the front yard. Your meeting with the Realtor should occur within 24 hours of owning the property and then you put it on the market for sale by owner. You don't want to list with a Realtor right away because chances are you have some repairs to make to the property. Once the repairs are mostly complete and the property is starting to look nice, you can list with a Realtor then; but in the meantime, you will start by selling on your own. On the sign you will be tempted to use one of those information tubes that hold a sheet of paper the prospective buyer can take that tells them about the property. If you use the information tube, you will decrease the number of calls you will get.

To get the forms discussed in this book and an additional free gift, visit www.fastcashforms.com

You may be thinking why would I want to talk to all these people when they are just going to ask me questions about the house that I could have put on the information sheet. Remember you are in the marketing business. You want to capture all of the information on every potential buyer you can. If you use the information tube, you can't track who took a flyer. The only ones that call from the flyer are the ones most interested. The ones that were not interested are not interested in that house but what about the other house you have for sale or what about the house that you will buy in the near future? Having a good pool of qualified buyers is the key to selling quickly. Build a database to track these buyers and find out what they are looking for and what their price range is.

Have these prospective buyers work with your mortgage broker. This way you will know they were qualified correctly and this will give you more control of the transaction.

Another reason you will put the FSBO sign in the front yard is because you want to make sure people know the property is available and you want as much exposure as you can get. There may be people in the neighborhood that might have been on the lookout for a house in the area for a friend or relative to move into. In addition, you never know who might drive by while it is being rehabbed. Also, you may also be able to sell the property as is.

Formulate two prices the "as is" price and the price after repairs. Many people are willing to do the repairs themselves and will pay more for the property than you did because they will do the work themselves. Using this technique will increase your profits by thousands of dollars by saving you the realtors fee and by reducing your holding time and costs on the property.

To get the forms discussed in this book and an additional free gift, visit www.fastcashforms.com

When do the Repairs Start?

You want to start the planning of the repairs prior to the purchasing the property. During the time between when you get it under agreement and when you close you will show contractors the property and get an estimate of the repairs. Prior to the closing, select the contractors you will use and meet them at the property one or two days prior to closing.

During this meeting you will confirm with them the work that needs to be done and make sure they are prepared to get started the next day. Most contractors will be scheduled to start your job two to three weeks from the day your hire them. You want them in there the day after you own the property. Having them in there right from the start will serve two purposes. It will get the repairs done faster and the contractors can act as a selling agent for you.

Tell all your contractors that if a potential buyer walks into the house while they are there, show them around the house and if they buy, I will give them a $500 to $1,000 bonus. Most contractors are proud of their work and will want to show it off. Make sure that the contractor gets the prospective buyer's name and contact information so you will know who to pay for the lead and you will have their information to follow up with them.

What repairs do I focus on 1st?

Curb appeal is where you need to start. If they don't like the outside they will never make it to the inside. Focus on the following areas: roof, gutters, windows, siding, doors, driveway, and landscaping. The sooner you address the curb appeal, the more buyers you will have

To get the forms discussed in this book and an additional free gift, visit www.fastcashforms.com

calling you. The good news is that while the exterior is being worked on, the interior work can be happening at the same time. As you focus on the interior you want to appeal to the buyer's senses, specifically touch. The first thing they will touch will be the front door knob. Make sure the door knob is nice and that the door unlocks and opens easily.

Anything else they touch needs to be special such as light switches, interior door knobs, and faucets. Spending a few cents or a few dollars on these items will help the potential buyer have a better feel for the quality of your house. You will want to focus most of your attention on the areas of the kitchen and bathroom because these are the two areas that sell houses. People spend most of their waking hours in one of these two rooms. When it comes to floors and walls, keep the colors neutral and get some suggestions from Realtors on what buyers are looking for.

Make sure the basement is neat and that the heating system has been cleaned. Secure any hanging wires and make sure there is lots of light. Clear all the cobwebs from the joist bays and be sure to treat any odors. Create a system for yourself in regard to what repairs you make and in what order. Also track what materials you use and use the same materials over and over. This system will save you time and allow you to make more money.

Marketing to your Retail Buyer's List

So you have put the FSBO sign out front and don't have a buyer yet. Now it's time to show the property to your buyers. I typically wait to show any of the buyers on my retail buyers list until the property is 90% complete. This doesn't mean that I wait to tell them about the house until it is almost complete. Contact them right after you buy the house and confirm that they are still looking and find out if

To get the forms discussed in this book and an additional free gift, visit www.fastcashforms.com

anything has changed since the last time you spoke with them such as price, motivation, must haves in a house, etc.

You can tell them about the property but let them know that you can't get them inside just yet. Don't give them the address right away but wait a week or so until the house has some curb appeal and they can't wait to get in. Give them the address and if they don't call you right away after they drive by, then follow up with them. Let them know you should be able to get them in soon.

There are several methods to build your buyers list. One of the best methods is to hold a buyer's seminar. Everyone wants some free information on how to buy a house. See if you can get a local restaurant or church to allow you to have a meeting there for free or a small fee or donation.

Advertise the seminar by sending post cards to renters living in apartments in the area where you buy and sell. Use a classified ad as well as radio spots to market the seminar. Put up flyers at various locations around town like the supermarket, restaurants with cork boards, and any store with high traffic. To help you with the cost, you can invite a home inspector, an attorney, and a mortgage broker and have them pay some or all of your costs to put on the seminar.

They will each speak on their part of the home buying process and provide discounts on their services. You will then talk about the property or properties that you have for sale and you can even show them some of the houses you sold in the past so they can see the quality product you put out. You may get a buyer right there at the seminar or it may create a competition atmosphere.

The ones that are not interested in your properties will go on your buyers list for future properties. Follow with all attendees to

To get the forms discussed in this book and an additional free gift, visit www.fastcashforms.com

further qualify them and verify the information they provided. Be sure to have a sign in sheet for all attendees.

Choose your Neighbor Campaign

Another method of attracting buyers is the "Choose your Neighbor Campaign". Send post cards or flyers to all the houses in the neighborhood. On the flyer or post card you can announce an open house and invite them to it. There is nothing better than a buyer hearing from a neighbor how great the area is and what makes the neighborhood so great.

Classifieds

Classified ads work as well. You can place two types of ads. The first type is property specific and the only people who will respond are the people interested in that specific property. The other type is a direct response advertisement. This type is designed for everyone who reads it to call. If you are going to spend money on marketing, you might as well capture as many buyers as possible.

Your ad can be specific to first time home buyers and offer a free report on how to avoid the pitfalls when buying your first home. Create a headline that captures their attention like, limited time home ownership programs with 100% financing.

Describe the property with words like recently updated, excellent area or great schools. At the end of the ad, tell them what to do. "Call now". You have a few choices on how to capture the calls. They can go to you, an answering service, your assistant, or a toll free 24 hour per day voice mail. Your best choices will be anything but you. Your time is more valuable. The voicemail is a good option because you will capture the number they are calling from and the

To get the forms discussed in this book and an additional free gift, visit www.fastcashforms.com

voicemail can be set up to provide them with instructions as to how to get more information. Make sure that you follow up with the people who call but don't call back after they drive past the property.

Websites

Websites are another way to market for buyers and market your properties. You may have a website to attract motivated sellers, but you want a separate website to attract motivated buyers. Put your website on all of your advertising: signs, ads, flyers, and information sheet. You can post your properties for sale on the website and capture their information to add to your database. Put pictures of the property on the website showing the best features of the house or property.

Flyers

Another inexpensive way to market your property is using flyers. The cost of creating and distributing is minimal so this will be one of the least costly methods. It can be very effective but it will depend upon the placement. You can create your own or use a copy center to make you hundreds of copies in just minutes. Use some sort of colored paper but do not go overboard on ultra bright. You want something that will stand out yet be professional.

You will want to spread your flyers around town at places where potential buyers might see them. Visit the local businesses around your property and ask to post one at the checkout counter or maybe they have a bulletin board.

You can put them in a supermarket, convenience store, barber shop and beauty salon, diner, and sandwich shop. One of the best places will be at the apartment buildings near the property. Stop by the rental office and see if they will let you leave some. In almost all cases

To get the forms discussed in this book and an additional free gift, visit www.fastcashforms.com

this will not be possible. You may have better luck putting the flyers in the common areas of the apartment complex such as the mail box area, laundry room, garage, workout room, or pool. You also should send them to all the local Realtor offices. When the Realtor calls you make sure they know that your price doesn't include a commission. You could also tell them to add 2% to the price and that is what you are willing to pay them. Most Realtors don't mind as long as they know the arrangement up front.

Be prepared as they will try to get a listing from you rather than present a buyer but stick to your system and let them know that you are not ready to list the property. When you interview the Realtor on the first day you own the property, you should tell them about your marketing system and that the property will have a for sale by owner sign and that you will be doing other marketing such as flyers. If you explain ahead of time they will not be surprised and know that they still have a chance at listing the property.

How to Show the Property

As soon as the repairs on your property are complete you can begin to show the property to prospective buyers. One of the last steps of the rehab process is to have the house cleaned top to bottom. Although you have new carpet and freshly painted walls, there is a certain amount of construction dust that will build up. Make sure the windows sparkle and the toilets and tubs and sinks are gleaming. All garbage and dumpsters should be gone and when showing the property at night make sure all the lights are on. As far as the exterior goes, make sure you plan to have the grass mowed weekly.

As you show potential buyers the property, you should direct them where certain rooms are and how to get around the house. You should remain nearby so if they have any questions, you will be there to

To get the forms discussed in this book and an additional free gift, visit www.fastcashforms.com

answer them. Try not to follow too closely as they may want a moment of time alone to discuss something. Your best option is to tell them where you will be in the house and just call for you if they need you.

Staging the House

To give yourself every chance to win over that buyer you want the house to feel like a home. You can bring furniture in the house. The best rooms for furniture would be dining room or the kitchen. The living room is also an option. To make the house seem more like a home you should stage the kitchen and bathroom. Remember, these are the rooms that sell the house. In the bathroom you can put a floor mat, a shower curtain, a hand towel, a soap dish with soap, fill the toilet paper roll, tissue box, and tooth brush holder.

As far as the kitchen you can bring in some flowers, a cookbook, pot holders, dish towel, magnets on the fridge, and a knife set. Inside the refrigerator put a champagne bottle with a bow on it that says CONGRATULATIONS.

They will open the refrigerator and they will see the bottle. This is powerful because now you are playing on their emotions. Purchasing a home is already emotional and that bottle of champagne just pulled them in a little closer. As they open the refrigerator, they are imagining themselves celebrating after closing on the house. Depending on the season, plant flowers in the front of the house or place a few hanging pots. Make sure you go to the house once a week to water the flowers.

Prequalifying Buyers

As you start to market the property you will find a number of interested parties. However, not all of these people have the ability to

To get the forms discussed in this book and an additional free gift, visit www.fastcashforms.com

purchase your property. Prior to showing them the property you must pre-qualify them. If you choose not to do this you will waste a lot of time showing your property to people who could never buy it.

You have two pre-qualifications methods:

1. Ask the buyer if they are working with a mortgage broker. If they are working with a mortgage broker then ask if they have been pre-approved. If they have, find out for how much. They should also have a pre-qualification letter. If they are not working with a mortgage broker, they need to be prior to seeing the property.

You can tell them to go back to the mortgage broker they are working with and get pre-qualified or you can have them work with the mortgage broker on your team. Try to have them work with your mortgage broker because that will give you better control over the transaction.

2. Your other option is to ask them some questions such as:
    A. What is their current housing situation?
    B. Are they currently employed?
    C. Do they have the money for the down payment?
    D. How good is their credit?
    E. Is this house in their price range?

Based on the answers you may feel comfortable showing them the house. If you qualify them yourself, be sure to find out what mortgage broker they are working with and see if they would be open to using yours.

Offers

To get the forms discussed in this book and an additional free gift, visit www.fastcashforms.com

As you show the property, you may have an interested buyer. They may even make you a verbal offer on the spot. You should not negotiate the price verbally but instead should have the offer in writing. The reason you should not negotiate verbally is because they will see your body language and you may tip your hat as to what you would be willing to go down to. Tell them what your asking price is and let them know that you will entertain all reasonable offers but they need to be written.

Don't send them away to write the offer and expect them to come back because they may not. Have some blank real estate purchase and sales agreements with you or keep some at the property. Tell them to complete the form and prepare a check for the earnest money deposit.

There are several techniques you can use when they want to negotiate. One strategy is to decline all offers and provide no counter offer. This is effective on offers that are a little in the low side and you want them to raise their offer quite a bit. In most cases you will have them negotiating against themselves and they will raise their offer. If they don't raise their offer then after a few days you can counter at a price close to your asking price and keep the negotiations open. Another technique is to tell everyone you are accepting offers until Sunday at 5pm and will make a decision on which offer to accept Sunday night.

You have just created a horse race and if they are the only ones that put in an offer that is called a phantom horse race. A phantom horse race because they assumed that they were competing against other buyers. Most of the time this will cause them to put in a higher offer than they normally would of if you didn't use this technique. Even if they offer full price, make sure that you don't look too excited.

To get the forms discussed in this book and an additional free gift, visit www.fastcashforms.com

List with a Realtor

You have tried to sell the property on your own but your buyers' list is not interested.

It is time to list it with a Realtor. Call the Realtor you liked the best based on the visit they had with you at the property the day you bought it. Have them meet you at the property and tell them the house is just about finished and you are considering listing. Upon arriving at the house show the Realtor around and ask them what they think of the house now that it is complete. Confirm with them the market conditions and what the 30 day price is for the house. If all goes well they will ask you to sign a listing agreement.

The type of agreement will most likely be an exclusive listing agreement. Under that agreement they will get paid a commission no matter who buys the property. Most of the terms of the agreement are pre-printed and not negotiable. There are a few terms that are negotiable such as sales commission and the term of the agreement. In regards to the commission you should pay a 5% commission.

You can also offer a 1% bonus if a contract is accepted within the first seven days and the buyer closes on the property. In regards to the term or length of the agreement, you do not want to sign any exclusive listing that has a term of more than 90 days. If they insist on six months, you need to move on to someone else. If you don't have it sold in three months, you need to re-evaluate the situation and try another Realtor.

If you have some potential buyers that have not made an offer but you feel they might after the property is listed with the Realtor, list

To get the forms discussed in this book and an additional free gift, visit www.fastcashforms.com

them on the listing contract as exclusions. This mean that if one of the excluded persons buys the property, the Realtor will not be due a commission.

ACCEPTING OFFERS

The only offers that you will consider are those that are written and have an earnest money deposit attached to them. When it comes to evaluating offers, you need to consider more than price.

Other areas of negotiation include:

1. Closing date
2. Inspection Period Duration
3. Earnest Money Deposit Amount
4. Mortgage Contingency Clause
    A. Date to provide commitment letter or denial
    B. Terms of Mortgage
        (I) Interest rate
        (II) Percentage down
        (III) Number of points
        (IV) Term of loan
5. Any special provisions they write into the contract

Closing Date

They will want it as far out as possible and you want it as soon as possible. You should keep it under 60 days and try for 45 days.

Inspection Date

The inspection should happen within a week of the contract and the results and any requests should be made within five days of inspection.

Ernest Money Deposit

Get as much as you can and typically 3-5% of the purchase price. Most contracts will have some contingencies so the amount won't matter until the contingencies expire but get a good amount up front so they are locked into the deal.

Mortgage Contingency Clause

The most important part here is to have a short date or short period of time between the date you accept the agreement and the date they must provide a written acceptance or denial from a lender. Speak with their mortgage broker or lender and ask them how long it should take. Make sure that this date is no more than 30 days from the date of the contract so if they are unable to get the loan commitment, you will cancel the contract and move on to another buyer.

Terms of the Mortgage

In this section you want them to have put current rates, current points and at least 10% down if not 20% depending on what type of financing available. If they put current rates and current points they will not be able to back out of the contract if the rates increase. If they specify a rate not to exceed "X" and the rate is above "X", they will be able to cancel the contract and get their money back. Just make sure whatever is in this section that it is reasonable and likely that the rates won't change so much and let them out of the contract.

Special Provisions

To get the forms discussed in this book and an additional free gift, visit www.fastcashforms.com

Be wary of any special provisions written into the contract. The typical ones have to do with something they want you to leave in the house at the time of closing such as appliances or something they want you to remove such as a pile of logs or a workbench in the basement or an old boat in the side yard.

Signing the Contract

At this point, the contract seems in order and you are willing to accept it. Should you sign it? Do not sign any contract unless you have it reviewed by an attorney. Before signing you will require a pre-qualification or pre-approval letter from the mortgage broker or lender the buyer intends to use. Inform the buyer that you need to speak to the lender or mortgage broker to ask some follow up questions prior to accepting or signing the agreement.

If they ask you what you need to know, tell them you have some further questions about the type of loan program the mortgage broker will put them into. If they tell you that they don't want you to call or the mortgage broker refuses to answer your questions, tell them that you can't accept the contract until they agree to put us in contact with the mortgage broker.

The reason you need to speak to the mortgage broker or lender is to find out what the title seasoning requirement will be for the loan they are applying for. Title seasoning refers to the number of days the seller has owned the property. Some lenders have a requirement of 30 days, 90 days, 6 months, or one year. In most cases you will have been on title as the owner for less than six months and if you have followed the timelines properly, you have probably owned it for less than 60 days.

To get the forms discussed in this book and an additional free gift, visit www.fastcashforms.com

The question you want to ask the mortgage broker is as follows: "Can you read to me what the underwriting guideline says in regards to title seasoning for the loan program you are putting the buyer's into?" In most cases they won't know what you are talking about but that doesn't mean they are a bad broker. The typical property that they lend on has been seasoned for more than what the guidelines say, so they have probably have never dealt with it. Tell them, it is okay if they are not sure but to check with their manager or the lender to see what the underwriting guidelines say. In most cases, there won't be an issue with the title seasoning.

Depending on the lender they may require you to produce receipts and cancelled checks for the work that was done to the property and then they will limit the amount of profit you are able to make on the property. You don't want to go down that road so only work with buyers when the title seasoning is not going to be an issue at all.

If you fail to take this step, you most likely will not find out about the title seasoning issue until a week or a few days prior to the closing. This is because most mortgage underwriters do not look at the entire package until they have all of the information in front of them and are ready to fund the loan. It is one of those minor details that will come back to haunt you if you don't deal with it properly.

The contract has been reviewed and the terms are acceptable to you and the buyer. Don't celebrate yet because you have a few more hoops to jump through. The hoops will be the contingency dates in the contract. Go through the contract and pull out all the important dates.

These dates include:
1. Date to make application with a lender
2. Inspection date

To get the forms discussed in this book and an additional free gift, visit www.fastcashforms.com

3. Inspection report date
4. Mortgage commitment date
5. Closing date

Put these dates in your calendar so that you can stay on top of the process and keep the wheels moving. Even if you are using a Realtor, you should still stay on top of it even if they say that they are on top of it. They will only lose part of the commission and you stand to lose $20,000 to $50,000+.

To get the forms discussed in this book and an additional free gift, visit www.fastcashforms.com

Chapter 15: Taking The Next Step

  At this point, you may now realize that there is a lot of money to be made in the real estate investment game. We quickly learned, at the start of our real estate investing careers, the more we learned, the more we earned.

  If you would like additional resources or if you would like a personal coach to help you reach your real estate goals faster, you can contact us at the office at 781-878-7114.

  You are about to embark on a journey that can create financial freedom for you and your family and it can happen in a very short period of time.

  Call us when you are having difficulties and we will help you break through your obstacles. Call us when you accomplish your triumphs and we will celebrate with you!!!

  Here at **Creative Success Alliance**, we now consider you a part of the family and we are here to support you during this wondrous journey of real estate investing!!

To get the forms discussed in this book and an additional free gift, visit www.fastcashforms.com

www.ingramcontent.com/pod-product-compliance
Lightning Source LLC
Chambersburg PA
CBHW070824250426
43671CB00036B/2065